SALMON

SALMON

a cookbook *by Diane Morgan*

PHOTOGRAPHS BY DIANE MORGAN, FOOD PHOTOGRAPHS BY E.J. ARMSTRONG

foreword by John Ash

CHRONICLE BOOKS
SAN FRANCISCO

To Greg, my globetrotting salmon research companion—
I couldn't ask for a more wonderful mate

Text copyright © 2005 by Diane Morgan.
Photographs copyright © 2005 by Diane Morgan and E.J. Armstrong.

Library of Congress Cataloging-in-Publication Data available.

ISBN 0-8118-4212-6

Manufactured in Singapore.

Prop stylist: Curtis Steiner
Food stylists: Patty Wittmann and Diana Isaiou
Photography assistant: Scott Pitts

Design: Annabelle Gould

Distributed in Canada by Raincoast Books
9050 Shaughnessy Street
Vancouver, British Columbia V6P 6E5

10 9 8 7 6 5 4 3 2 1

Chronicle Books LLC
85 Second Street
San Francisco, California 94105

www.chroniclebooks.com

ABOVE, LEFT TO RIGHT
Toward Laerdal, Sognefjorden, Norway; fish market,
Bergen, Norway; along the Sognefjorden, Norway

PAGE 8, CLOCKWISE FROM LEFT
Mike Peterson, Wester Ross Salmon Farm, Ullapool,
Scotland; Ullapool, Scotland; Sognefjorden, Norway;
Bergen, Norway

PAGE 12, TOP TO BOTTOM
Kent Herschleb fishing for salmon on the Savonia
Cordova, Alaska; near Cordova, Alaska

PAGE 13
Arriving via railroad in Flåm, Norway

PAGE 14, CLOCKWISE FROM BOTTOM LEFT
Wester Ross Salmon Farm, Ullapool, Scotland:
Author in a float suit, worker inspecting a salmon,
worker hand-feeding salmon

PAGE 15
Enroute to Ullapool, Scotland

ACKNOWLEDGMENTS   In so many ways *Salmon* has been the most extraordinary of all the books I've written. When I began writing the proposal for this book, I decided that I would need to step out of the kitchen and away from my computer and travel to truly appreciate salmon. Not only did I want to taste salmon preparations from near and far, but I wanted to fish for salmon, visit Alaska for the opening of the Copper River salmon season, journey to Lærdal to see the most famous salmon river in Norway, and, finally, visit a certified high-quality salmon farm on the northwest coast of Scotland. Every aspect of researching and writing this book has been a wonderful and incredible journey.

Bill LeBlond, my editor and dear friend, is clearly at the top of my list for helping me develop this project. With every book I have received such skilled professional guidance, support, and time. It's a professional relationship beyond compare and one I cherish deeply.

To Amy Treadwell, Michael Weisberg, Michele Fuller, Kendra Kallan, Leslie Jonath, and the others at Chronicle Books who have inspired, supported, publicized, and otherwise kept my projects on track—thank you, thank you—you are all absolutely delightful to work with. To Carolyn Miller, many thanks for copyediting another one of my books.

To Cheryl Russell, my fabulous assistant, I don't know what I'd do without you. You make the process of developing and testing recipes a pleasure and loads of fun. I believe we've both grown gills working on this book, and I wouldn't be surprised to find a few scales still sticking to our skin!

To my friends Harriet and Peter Watson, sharing our time together in Cordova, Alaska, was amazingly fun. Peter, thank you for all the gorgeous photographs and for taking my official author photo. But most of all, thank you for helping me reel in my 75-pound halibut. I can still hear your patient directions and words of confidence as I fought mightily to bring in my catch. And Harriet, I think we looked pretty darn cute in our matching fishing waders, fly rods over our shoulders, swishing our way through shallow water in pursuit of the perfect stream, bear sighting and all. There were so many "firsts" on this trip; it will always be a special memory.

To Kent "Curly" Herschleb and his terrific wife, Diane, I can't thank you enough for taking me on board (literally) and allowing me to experience firsthand what it's like to be an independent wild-salmon fisherman. All the connections you helped me make were invaluable in writing this book. To Sylvia Lange and her husband, Greg Meyer, thank you for making our stay in Cordova, Alaska, such a wonder. To Phil Oman on the *Bummaree,* Danny Carpenter and his little dog, Daisy, on the *Ambergris,* and Paul Hearn on the *SalmonMaster,* it was great to meet you and share a spectacular beer and salmon dinner on the deck. To John Bosch at Copper River Seafoods, thank you for processing and packing up all that salmon and halibut for me to air-ship home.

In Norway, I'd like to thank Lars Røtterud and Scott Givot for making our stay in Oslo such a fun and welcoming experience. Many thanks go to Helene Maristuen at the Norsk Villaks Senter in Lærdal for providing me with such a wealth of information.

In Scotland, many thanks to Julie Edgar, communications director for Scottish Quality Salmon, for all your tireless help and coordination of my trip. Special thanks to Gilpin Bradley of Wester Ross Salmon, Ltd. for showing me how salmon can be farmed responsibly to achieve a high-quality product.

In addition, many thanks to Hugh Richards, Alistair MacLeod, and Mike Peterson, also of Wester Ross Salmon, for helping me understand all the quality-assurance factors involved in farming salmon.

Close to home, many thanks to all my friends and colleagues: Kate Morrison and Dave McElroy, Margie and Ken Sanders, Steve and Marci Taylor, Roxane and Austin Huang, Turid Owren, Pat Monroe, Paul Scardina, Summer Jameson, Audrey and Willie Anderson, Laurie and Peter Turney, Peter and Michelle Trumbo, Kam and Tony Kimball, Mary and Jack Barber, Sara and Erik Whiteford, Tori Ritchie, Josie Jimenez, Lorinda and Ray Moholt, Paola Gentry and Eric Watson, Tom Giese, Dennis Katayama, and all the folks involved with Salmon Nation. Many thanks to Eric Gorrell and Mike DeMarte at Liner & Elsen wine store in Portland for all their help with the wine suggestions.

Special thanks to David Watson for not only sampling my recipes and giving me genuine feedback but calling and saying, "Diane, I just caught four steelhead. Do you want one?" David, I promise you, the answer will always be "Yes!"

Finally, this book wouldn't have been nearly as much fun to research without my loving and support-ive husband, Greg, sharing in all my travel adventures. To Eric and Molly, my children, thank you for all your love and support every step of the way. And, Molly, I am now done developing and testing salmon recipes, so you won't need to say, "Oh, Mom, not salmon *again*."

FOREWORD   I share Diane's awe of salmon. I first came to know this magnificent fish when, as a little kid, I went fishing with my father in northern California. Wild-salmon season opens in early spring, when the fish begin their migration back to their freshwater birthplace. We'd get our gear together, book ourselves on a boat, and head out into the usually very foggy, very rolling seas off San Francisco's Golden Gate. I've never forgotten this annual ritual of fishermen and fish. This was when I first began to understand and appreciate the annual dramas that occur in nature and their connection to what we eat. Any of us who have been lucky enough to grow up in a food-producing or -gathering family I suspect also share this appreciation of nature's rhythms.

This drama profoundly affected what I chose to do later in life as a chef. I have long espoused (as have many others) that food is best when it is gathered or harvested during its prime season, as close to home as possible, and in as natural and pristine a state as we can find it. It's what I call "ethical" food and has been a mantra of mine since I opened my namesake restaurant in Sonoma County, California, nearly twenty-five years ago.

An unfortunate fact, at least in my mind, is that many of us have no real idea of how our food comes to us. We live in a time when almost everything is seemingly available to us all year round. Nature's rhythms, if we were ever aware of them, have been forgotten for the most part. Diane's book gently reminds us that eating is a direct act of participation in these cycles and rhythms, whether we are conscious of that or not. I call your attention especially to her discussion on the merits of wild versus farmed salmon. Several recent reports and articles have raised both ecological and health concerns about farm-raised salmon. Diane provides an evenhanded look at this controversy and helps us to understand how to make responsible choices.

Some of us may never go fishing for salmon, but if you are lucky enough to do so, Diane has even included a brief primer on how to clean and prepare a whole salmon. More important though is her description of what to look for in buying salmon and how to handle and store it. Even though you no doubt bought this book for the recipes, read this section! It's important information that you can apply to the selection and storing of most fishes.

Now, on to the recipes. I can see and taste Portland (Diane's hometown) in them! For those of you who have never visited there, it's a wonderful city and one of my favorites. Green and lush as a result of its often rainy and damp weather, it has a rich agricultural history and consciousness. It has spawned several generations of creative chefs and home cooks, including Diane. You'll see influences of many cuisines in the recipes, which mirror Portland's ethnic diversity. All of the recipes in the book are terrific, but among my new favorites are Vietnamese Salad Rolls, Grilled Salmon Tacos with Chipotle Sauce, and Pan-Roasted Salmon with Warm French Lentil Salad. These three beautifully illustrate the cross-cultural flavors that Diane has deliciously captured. Brava, Diane!

—*John Ash, chef and award-winning author of* From the Earth to the Table *and* Cooking One on One

CONTENTS

INTRODUCTION

I'm hooked—fundamentally and permanently in love
with every aspect of salmon.

The legends and culture of the fish captivate me, their wondrous and complex life cycle amazes me, and salmon is a visual and savory delight to my senses. And, now, after my trip to Cordova, Alaska, I'm considering becoming an angler, and entering the world of sportfishing as a hobby! In this introduction, I'm sharing my stories and tales, hoping that what you gain from this book will be not only a great collection of salmon recipes, but also a glimpse into the world of salmon fishing and farming, its history, challenges, and rewards.

While in Cordova to do research for this book, I went sportfishing for the first time. My husband, Greg, and our close friends, Peter and Harriet Watson, tagged along on the trip, wanting to experience commercial salmon fishing as much as I did. On one of our free days, we hired a guide and went halibut fishing in Orca Bay. The cold gray waters, comfortably calm that day, lapped against a rugged shoreline where the water met an alpine world of forested hillsides. Above were commanding views of glaciers and rocky spires. Truly, sitting in the boat watching this land of untouched wilderness and beauty was all I needed. But I was handed a rod with baited hook, and shown how to cast my line. I serenely waited for a bite, reeling in and replacing bait every time those clever fish snared the bait off the hook and swam away. Peter caught a fish; Harriet got a bite and landed a respectably sized halibut; and I baited again and waited. I was told a true fisherman never gives up hope, and my patience was rewarded. I believe I said, "Peter, something's on my line and, whoa, I think he's headed to shore." Leaning back, pressing my feet into the side of the boat for leverage, I engaged every arm muscle I had ever pumped at the gym and followed instructions. "Pull up, pull up, reel in, reel in, pull up, reel in, keep going, good," was the constant mantra from the guide and Peter. Harriet laughed and I held on. At the end of the struggle, and at the end of the line, was the biggest, ugliest halibut I had ever seen. (Halibut are not good-lookin' fish.) A day's work, a beer deserved, and, of course, pictures were taken. If that's what fishing is all about, even though my first catch wasn't a chinook or sockeye, I want more.

Researching wild salmon was my mission for this trip, and indeed, it was a mission accomplished. Kent Herschleb, known as "Curly" in Cordova, heads to Alaska every summer to join a fleet of independent commercial fishermen plying the waters of the Copper River delta for wild salmon. I've gotten to know Kent because his wife, Diane, teaches English at the high school my children attend. When Kent heard I was writing a book on salmon he invited me to visit Cordova and spend time on his boat.

We flew to Cordova the second week in May, right after the first "opener" of the salmon run. Salmon fishing in Alaska is tightly regulated and managed for sustainability by the Alaska Department of Fish and Game to ensure that a daily quota of "escaped" salmon make it upstream to spawn. A sonar station 30 miles upriver, at the Million Dollar Bridge, tracks the runs. If enough fish are making it upstream to spawn, fishermen are given a period of time to fish, an "opener," usually 12 to 24 hours, before stopping to allow the upriver count to rise again.

Leaving the dock in Cordova at 4 A.M. we "commuted" about 2 hours out to the Copper River Delta, a 700,000-acre wetland of sloughs and rivers. The Copper River delta, roughly 50 miles wide at its mouth and 275 miles long, begins on the north slope of the Wrangell Mountains in Alaska's interior. Adult salmon, primarily king and sockeye, begin returning from the Gulf of Alaska in early May to battle their way upstream to spawn.

Carefully maneuvering the shallow channels, Kent sized up the waters and idled his 30-foot fiberglass vessel, the *Savonia,* in what he thought might be a good spot. His boat is a bow picker, because the reel that hauls in the drift gill net is at the bow of the boat. These boats require only one person to operate. We were along for the ride, observing only, not allowed (by licensing laws) to help or handle any of the gear. Releasing a lever, Kent began feeding out almost 900 feet of curtainlike net into the water, suspended from a float line at the surface and a weighted line along the submerged bottom edge. The net's mesh openings are just large enough to allow an adult fish head to get through and become entangled at the gills.

The waiting game began, with a keen watch for the floats sinking, indicating that something was caught in the net. When the lever is pulled back, the net winds over the bow, the mesh wet and glistening as it rhythmically threads over the roller. Cautiously watching the net, Kent stopped rewinding as soon as he saw a salmon caught and thrashing in the net. Every king caught adds up to a good day; every sockeye adds to the bottom line. Each salmon hauled in was immediately bled and placed in a holding tank filled with shaved ice. With the net emptied and fully reeled in, we put the boat in gear and changed location. The work was continuous for as long as the opener lasted, which was 12 hours.

Kent is in cahoots with about five other fishermen, all agreeing to be supportive of one another, in pursuit of successful catches. With time off between openers, they have developed a secret code so they can radio one another regarding prime fishing spots, types of salmon being caught, and any problems with weather and ocean conditions. Regular dispatches from one boat to another go something like this: "I'm drinking a Schlitz at Roswell and got a muffin." Because they change their codes every year, I won't be giving anything away to tell you that message means, "The fishing is average at Kokenhenik and 10 sockeye are caught."

Fishing for wild Alaskan salmon is tough, competitive work, and unpredictable as a source of income. Trying to maintain prices with the pressure of cheap, farmed salmon flooding the market challenges the livelihood of the fishermen as well as the coastal communities.

Traveling to Oslo, Norway, I found our journey by train and then ferry to Lærdal breathtakingly beautiful. Every vista looked as stunning as the images on picture postcards. About halfway between Oslo and Bergen, my husband, Greg, and I transferred trains in order to pick up the Flåm railroad. This rail line descends steeply, making hairpin turns, past glacier-fed waterfalls and through long, blasted rock tunnels to the tiny town of Flåm. We spent the night in order to meet the morning ferry headed to Lærdal. The quaint town of Lærdal sits at the spot where the Lærdal River flows into the Sognefjorden, the longest fjord in Norway. On this June morning, the water was still and turquoise blue, the cloud cover was breaking, and what were glimpses of blue turned to large patches of blue as we sailed. The shoreline, gently sloped in places with meadows for grazing, quickly turned to steep slopes densely covered with trees. Where trees could no longer grow, rocky outcrops appeared, and the mountains soared upwards to snow-capped peaks.

The Lærdal River is the longest river in Norway and the most famous salmon river in the country. This is where King Harald of Norway comes to fish, as does Prince Charles and Eric Clapton. Fishing is restricted, reservations are difficult to obtain, and if you are lucky enough to secure a license for a day, it will cost you 10,000 kroner, or approximately $1,500 (U.S.), calculating current exchange rates. However, there is only a minimal charge to visit the Norwegian Wild Salmon Centre (Norsk Villaks Senter), and that's what we did.

The Norwegian Wild Salmon Centre is located on the banks of the Lærdal River. It was opened by His Majesty King Harald on June 15, 1996. The Centre provides insight into the life and legends of the Atlantic salmon and informs its visitors about the protection, management, and exploitation of the wild salmon stocks. Wild Atlantic salmon and sea trout can be viewed swimming through the fish ladders, a documentary film explains the status of wild salmon in Norway, and there are extensive scientific and cultural exhibits. The Centre is dedicated to the preservation of wild salmon in Norway. Salmon stocks are severely depleted in this region, due to overfishing, destruction of habitat, and the disease and inbreeding caused by farmed salmon. Scientists and conservationists have made a concerted effort to bring public awareness to these issues. The Centre supports those interests.

Traveling from Norway to Scotland, we flew to Aberdeen and meandered by car to Inverness, staying two nights. From there we drove over hills and dales, dodging sheep at every turn, until we finally hit the rugged coastline of northwestern Scotland and the tiny town of Ullapool. The accents were thick and the street signs were written in both English and Gaelic.

By contacting Scottish Quality Salmon, I was able to visit the salmon farm of one of its members. One of the owners of Wester Ross Salmon, Ltd. is J. R. G. Bradley—Gilpin Bradley, as we were introduced. Gilpin's father started the first fish farm in Scotland. Established in 1977, Wester Ross Salmon is Scotland's oldest independent fully integrated salmon farmer, handling all stages of the production process from egg to fully prepared salmon fillet. Wester Ross operates four freshwater farms and three seawater farms on the northwest coast and a processing facility in Dingwall. As Gilpin explains, "Our principal objective is to have the highest standards of salmon welfare in Scotland and care for Scotland's environment. This will ensure that we are producing the finest quality Scottish salmon. Salmon farmers are guardians of the natural environment, since our livelihoods depend entirely on caring for the pristine waters where our salmon grow. Scotland has many significant environmental benefits; jeopardizing this position would be very shortsighted."

To help me understand how salmon could be farmed to the highest standards of fish welfare and environmental care, Gilpin, along with his longtime employee, Hugh Richards, fitted Greg

and me with float suits and boated us out to the fish pens in the protected sea loch. Hugh explained the many points that distinguish their operation from large multinational salmon-farming operations.

At Wester Ross, salmon nets are inspected daily, and in order to facilitate maximum water exchange, each population is moved into a clean net at approximately three-week intervals during the spring and summer months, and at six-week intervals during winter. The vacated net is left attached to the pen but hauled clear of the water to dry naturally in the sun. This allows a thorough inspection. Net damage is a very rare occurrence, and the risk of salmon escaping is minimized by using smaller pens. Salmon are fed by hand throughout their life, with control systems on most pens that indicate when the salmon have stopped feeding, thus minimizing the risk of waste feed. No growth promoters or chemical supplements are used. All sites are monitored on a continual basis for environmental impact, with a formal measuring of seabed impact taking place on an annual basis. And finally, Wester Ross farming methods are regulated by ten different statutory bodies and sixty-three pieces of legislation; Scottish salmon farmers are among the most highly regulated farmers in the world.

Mike Peterson, another longtime employee and manager of the sea pens we visited, says, "I grew up in a family that has been fishing the sea for generations. By the early 1980s, as the fish stocks became depleted, many in the area became unemployed. When fish farming came into the area, I had a lot of reservations in terms of what kind of employer these salmon farmers might be, whether th̶ ̶f̶arms would be good for the environment, and whether I would feel good about feeding this f̶ ̶ ̶ ̶ ̶ ̶ ̶ ̶ ̶ ̶ ̶ ̶ ̶ ̶ ̶ ̶Part of why I feel good about being with Wester Ross is because I can mak̶ ̶ ̶ ̶ ̶ ̶ ̶ ̶ ̶ ̶ ̶ ̶ ̶ ̶ ̶ ̶U̶llapool where I grew up, feel good that my work doesn't h̶ ̶ ̶ ̶ ̶ ̶ ̶ ̶ ̶ ̶ ̶ ̶bout feeding this salmon to my family."

̶ ̶ ̶ ̶ ̶ ̶ ̶ ̶ing to Ullapool for the evening, we ̶ ̶ ̶ ̶ ̶urselves by the fire with a glass of Scotch, ̶ ̶ ̶ ̶locally farm-raised salmon for dinner, ̶ ̶ ̶e bar afterwards listening to a band from ̶ ̶tral Highlands playing classic Scottish ̶ ̶and smiled, realizing that we had met some ̶most remarkable folks in one of the farthest ̶ers of Scotland.

My global jaunt in search of the salmon story, ̶lding the context of this book and inspiring the ̶cipes I developed, has been a life-transforming ̶xperience for me. I've traveled to remote places

wher̶ ̶ ̶ ̶ ̶ ̶ ̶ ̶ ̶ ̶ion, made lasting friends with people I would not have̶ ̶ ̶ ̶ ̶ ̶ ̶ ̶ ̶derstanding of salmon, a glorious species that we nee̶ ̶ ̶ ̶ ̶ ̶ ̶ ̶

̶ ̶ ̶ ̶ ̶ ̶to the kitchen, earmark recipes you want to try, and ̶ ̶ ̶ ̶ty with salmon as the focal point. Cookbook authors p̶ ̶ ̶ ̶ ̶ ̶ ̶grease-stained copies of their books! I urge you, as well, a̶ ̶ ̶ ̶n easy chair, and learn all about this glorious and complex ̶ ̶fe cycle; the variety of species; the controversy regarding ̶ ̶remarkable value as a protein source. My hope is that you ̶bout salmon as much as I enjoyed researching it. Finally, ̶ount of salmon in order to write this book, it remains a fish I ̶d a bagel for Sunday brunch and I'm delighted, grilled salmon ̶and I never pass up a tray of hors d'oeuvres that includes ̶ou to try salmon in a myriad of ways—from smoked to grilled ̶d that you get as hooked as I am.

SALMON BASICS

1

In spring with the first melt water or flood the small salmon children migrate to the sea—they are then small and shining like herring—and they move on to the ocean and home to their parents living in the high seas. And when they are fully grown, they return to swim up in fresh water and streams, and increase their numbers by procreation, as well as to serve as food for man. And what is most fantastic of all, the salmon seeks the stream and the place where it was born.

From *On Animals, Fishes, Birds, and Trees of Norway* (1599), by Peder Claussøn Friis (1545–1614), a senior rector and the first Norwegian to describe the distinct characteristics of the life of a salmon

THE FANTASTIC LIFE OF SALMON

What a fantastic, legendary fish! What a complex, wondrous life! Salmon are anadromous fish, which means they are born in freshwater, migrate and spend most of their lives in saltwater, and then return to freshwater to spawn. The life cycle of a salmon is truly extraordinary. It begins in the fresh waters of a river and its tributaries, or in a lake with an outlet river. Here, the adults mate and lay eggs—as many as three to five thousand of them. The female turns on her side and, by bending her body and striking with her tail, creates a depression in the gravel of the streambed. This spawning nest is called a redd. The female salmon will make a series of redds and, in each, will deposit a portion of her eggs, which will be fertilized by the male partner. After all of her eggs have been deposited and fertilized, both female and male, with extremely rare exception, age rapidly and die.

When the eggs hatch, about four months later, the young fish (alevins) emerge from the gravel to feed and grow in the stream. These fish grow and develop until they are ready to begin their first migration down the tributaries to the river and finally out to sea. During migration, the young fish (parr) undergo a complex set of physiological changes that prepares them for living in saltwater. After these changes they are referred to as smolt. Salmon live in the ocean from one to five years, eating (and being eaten), and growing until they reach sexual maturity. The returning adults undergo a reverse set of physiological changes, allowing them to migrate from salt- to freshwater. The salmon swim hundreds of miles, returning to the river of their birth to spawn and then die, completing their life cycle.

What is it that directs the salmon to return, occasionally thousands of miles, from open ocean to the exact same tributary or lake where they were hatched, to spawn and create the next generation? Some scientists believe salmon have a navigational sense similar to migratory birds. In addition, they believe chemical imprinting during early development allows salmon to detect and home in on the unique chemical signature of not only the river of their birth but also the very gravel bed in that river or lake where they were conceived and from which they emerged to begin their amazing cycle of life.

UNDERSTANDING THE DIFFERENT TYPES OF SALMON

In the eighteenth century, Swedish botanist Linnaeus developed a Latin-based classification system for all living things grouped first by order, then family, then by genus, and finally by species. Every organism was identified by two Latin names *(binomen)*, the first name identified the genus and the second identified the species. (Your lessons from biology class may be a little rusty, but recall, as an easy example, that humans are *Homo sapiens*. Our genus is "*Homo*" and our species is "*sapien,*" meaning "man who is wise.") My reason for briefly explaining this classification system, of course, relates to salmon. Even though Atlantic and Pacific salmon look similar and are in the same family (Salmonidae) along with trout and Arctic char, they are, in fact, in different genera (the plural of *genus*).

Atlantic salmon belong to the genus *Salmo,* and interestingly enough, there is only one species *(salar)* of Atlantic salmon. Hence, all Atlantic salmon are classified as *Salmo salar. Salar* in Latin means "leaper," to best describe their athleticism in avoiding predators and their ability to jump waterfalls and rapids on the way back to their spawning grounds. Mature wild Atlantic salmon average about 10 pounds. They are sleek and muscular, with steel-blue backs covered with tiny black crosses. They are silver below the lateral line, with white bellies. The flesh of wild Atlantic salmon is firm and deep pink in color. The range of wild Atlantic salmon once extended from New York's Hudson all the way up the North Atlantic and arcing over to Russia's White Sea and down to the Douro River in Portugal. Many of these runs are now severely reduced or extinct due to industrialization, habitat loss, pollution, and overfishing by commercial fleets. The only wild Atlantic salmon available are those caught by sportfishermen. Almost all Atlantic salmon in the marketplace are farm-raised.

Pacific salmon belong to the genus *Oncorhynchus*. Unlike Atlantic salmon, there are seven species in this genus. Six species are native to North America. The seventh, masu salmon *(Oncorhynchus masou)* is found only off the coast of Japan and not included in this discussion.

Chinook, or king, salmon *(Oncorhynchus tschawytscha)* are truly the "kings" of all the Pacific salmon species, not only for their size but their economic value. The flavor and texture of the flesh is incomparable. King salmon can weigh over 100 pounds, but most weigh between 15 and 20 pounds and measure up to 36 inches in length. Hefty in appearance, king salmon are blue-green on the back and the top of the head, with silvery sides and white bellies. They have black spots on the upper half of their body and tail, plus distinctive black lower gums. The flesh of king salmon ranges from off-white to pinkish red. The rarely caught white-fleshed salmon have taken on a boutique status in the marketplace and are referred to as "ivory salmon." Kings range from Kotzebue Sound, Alaska, to Santa Barbara, California. Wild king salmon are available typically from mid–May until late September, though the famed and highly publicized Copper River salmon come into the marketplace in May and June. Not as popular for farming as other salmon species, farmed king salmon weigh between 5 and 15 pounds at harvest.

Coho, or silver, salmon *(Oncorhynchus kisutch)* come close to chinook in flavor but are smaller in size, ranging from 8 to 12 pounds in weight and 18 to 24 inches in length. Adult coho salmon are steel blue to light green, with silvery sides and white bellies. They have white gums, small black spots on the back, and are only lightly spotted at the top of the tail. The flesh of coho salmon is firmly textured and ranges from deep red to pinkish orange. Coho salmon occur naturally only in the Pacific Ocean and its tributaries from northern Alaska to as far south as Monterey Bay, California, though the stocks in Oregon and California are classified as threatened under the Endangered Species Act. The best catches of coho salmon are made between July and September, with a peak in August. Coho salmon are also farmed and sold at about 1 pound each.

Sockeye, or red, salmon *(Oncorhynchus nerka)* are long and slender, typically 5 to 12 pounds at maturity, with most weighing in at around 6 pounds. Their large, glassy, penetrating eyes distinguish them from coho salmon in the wild. Sockeye have spotless forest-green backs and bright silver bellies, and look almost glassy smooth, as though set in gel, when freshly caught. They have pale gums that bear no teeth, unlike a king or coho. At the spawning stage, the head of the sockeye will turn olive green while the body turns bright red. Though this is one of the reasons they are called "reds," it's also because of their distinctive flesh. Sockeye salmon have a bright deep-orange flesh with a high fat content that makes them prized, distinct, and delicious. Sockeye is the premium canned salmon variety and very popular for smoking. Though sockeye salmon range as far south as California, they are most abundant from the Columbia River northward, with large concentrations in British Columbia and Alaska. Wild sockeye salmon that do make it to market as unprocessed fish are typically available from late May to September.

Pink, or humpback, salmon *(Oncorhynchus gorbuscha)* are by far the most numerous of all the Pacific salmon species, representing a little over 50 percent of all salmon caught in Alaska. Pinks are typically 18 to 24 inches long and reach an average weight of 3 to 5 pounds. Pinks are steel-blue to blue-green with large black dots and silver sides. As the common name implies, the flesh is pale pink and lean, with a milder flavor than the other species. Pinks are widely used for canning, though pinks that make it to the market as unprocessed fish are typically sold as whole fish—and they're sold at bargain prices.

Chum salmon *(Oncorhynchus keta),* also called dog or keta, are slim and elongated, usually about 25 inches in length and averaging about 10 pounds in weight. Chums are steel blue on their backs and upper sides, without the fine black speckles of the other species. They have silvery white bellies. During spawning season, they develop elongated teeth, which is why the fish were given the common name "dog." The flavor, texture, and fat content of chum vary

considerably depending on where and when they are caught. Outside of Alaska, chum is sometimes sold under the label "keta." If chum are caught in the ocean when they are still feeding actively, the flavor and fat content of their flesh are at their best. Chum salmon in this condition—silvery skinned, almost like coho, with reddish flesh—are labeled "silver-brite" and command a higher price than "semi-brites" and "dark." As you might guess by the labeling, "semi-brites" have darker skin and paler flesh, and "darks" have the darkest skin and are noticeably paler and lower in fat. Chum salmon are commercially fished from Oregon to Alaska, but can be found in the Arctic Ocean, as well as in the Okhotsk and Bering Seas.

Steelhead salmon *(Oncorhynchus mykiss)* and rainbow trout used to be identified by the Latin name *Salmo gairdneri* and were considered part of the same genus as Atlantic salmon and various Eastern and European trout. However, scientists have argued for a long time that rainbow trout, and especially steelhead, have anatomical and behavioral traits that more closely match the Pacific salmons. In 1989, the American Fisheries Society approved and adopted this reclassification. Rainbow trout and steelhead are extremely similar. The only major difference is that steelhead are seagoing fish, while rainbow inhabit only freshwater. Steelhead average 12 to 18 inches in length and usually weigh between 5 and 9 pounds, though sportfishermen have caught steelhead as large as 36 pounds. They are silvery, with a number of small black spots. The flesh of this fish is usually bright red and rich or pink to white, depending on the diet. Steelhead and rainbow trout are rated one of the top five sport fish in North America. Wild steelhead are occasionally available in Northwest markets. In other parts of the world, what is labeled "steelhead" is rainbow trout raised on farms in saltwater.

WILD VS. FARMED SALMON: A HISTORY LESSON AND A CHALLENGE

Free-living Atlantic and Pacific salmon have been a valuable food source for thousands of years. Hunter-gatherer groups living along the coastal waters and major tributaries of North America caught what they needed while preserving the streams and waterways that produced their harvest. There is evidence of indigenous people having iconic relationships with salmon dating back twelve thousand years, from the Tlingits in Alaska to the Wyampum along the mighty Columbia River in the Pacific Northwest. Across the Atlantic, one of the oldest habitation sites in Ireland was discovered in 1972 at Mount Sandel, a bluff overlooking the River Bann. Careful analysis of evidence dating back to before 7000 B.C. has shown that hunter-gatherers there erected huts, gathered nuts, hunted boar, and speared salmon.

Fast-forwarding through the centuries, legislation was enacted to protect salmon by William the Lion, who ruled Scotland between 1165 and 1214. In the thirteenth century, Norwegian legislation known as the Gulating Law and the National Law of Magnus Lagabøter regulated fair fishing conduct. During the Industrial Revolution, pressures on European waterways, habitat destruction, and pollution severely compromised the survival of salmon. Up until about 1800, the Thames, the longest watercourse in England, was an excellent salmon river. Pollution decimated the salmon—the last salmon was caught in 1833—and in 1855 the river was so contaminated that no fish could survive. A similar tale is true of the Rhine River in Germany. Up until the end of the nineteenth century, the Rhine was considered the best salmon river in Europe. In the early 1900s, the salmon disappeared because of hydroelectric development and industrial pollution. The same pressures for industrial development and exploitation of energy resources were taking place in North America. Dams were being built, rivers were becoming polluted, and salmon populations were declining and, in some cases, becoming extinct.

As commercial fisherman became better skilled and better equipped, even more pressure was put on salmon stocks. Without international regulation, the amount of salmon caught led to overfishing, without concern for the sustainability of either the fish or future fishermen. Not enough salmon were making it back to their natal rivers to spawn, continuing their natural life cycle. The demand for salmon exceeded the supply, which led to the beginnings of salmon farming.

Though pioneers started researching and developing salmon farms in the 1960s, the industry really began in Norway in the early 1970s to help meet the growing demand for salmon in the marketplace. Scotland soon followed. Both of these areas were attractive as locations for fish pens because of the miles of coastline, much of it protected from storms. Protected coastal waters warmed by the Gulf Stream, with nearby rivers providing the freshwater needed to operate fish hatcheries, have been ideal for growing salmon. By 1985, technology had evolved so that farmers could raise almost 200 tonnes (metric tons) of salmon in pens that produced only a third of that amount the year before. As profits soared, a gold rush of sorts ensued. By 1986, approximately 635 salmon farms produced 45,675 tonnes of salmon; by 1990, production had grown to 146,000 tonnes.

With a glut of salmon on the market, prices fell. Salmon farmers from Scotland and Ireland accused the Norwegians of dumping salmon on the market below production costs, which led to an investigation by the European Union. As government restrictions were put into place, large aquaculture companies began exporting technology, equipment, and financing to other countries, the largest being Canada, the United States, and Chile. Today, one-third of the aquaculture industry is under the ownership of two large multinational companies, Nutreco and Fjord Cermaq.

In sharp contrast, Alaska, home to abundant stocks of salmon, is the only state in the nation whose constitution explicitly mandates that all fish, including salmon, shall be utilized, developed, and maintained on a sustained-yield basis. There are no salmon farms in Alaska. All Alaska salmon are wild, living in their natural habitat, growing to adulthood at their own pace, and eating marine life, which in turn colors each variety of salmon to its own hue. During the salmon season, biologists assess the returning salmon at key streams and rivers using sonar. Regulating and managing the salmon runs ensures that spawning salmon return in sufficient numbers to produce future generations. Alaska also strictly regulates the fisheries. A limited number of licensed fishermen using regulated fishing gear are allowed to fish in state waters up to three nautical miles offshore for limited periods of time.

The challenges of wild vs. farmed salmon are both environmental and economic. Salmon farming, like most intensive forms of producing food, has significant environmental costs. Escapement is a huge issue. Large numbers of salmon escape from sea pens both routinely and in severe weather. Interbreeding of escaped salmon undermines the genetic robustness of wild salmon and also infects wild salmon with parasites and diseases. In British Columbia, escaped Atlantic salmon, a farmed species not native to the Pacific waters, have populated at least three rivers. Diseases and infestations can spread rapidly to fish raised in overcrowded sea pens. Fish farmers combat these outbreaks using antibiotics, often resulting in disease-resistant bacteria being found in the intestines of farmed fish. Sea lice, which previously had been rarely found on the scales of wild juvenile salmon, are now regularly found there. Uneaten feed and feces from salmon accumulate beneath the sea pens, contaminating the water, depleting oxygen levels, and releasing noxious gases in decomposition.

Because the salmon-farming industry is controlled by just a handful of global corporations, they are able to flood the market with their product and force down prices. This puts an economic squeeze on the harvesters of wild salmon and the communities that depend on them. In coastal towns from California to Alaska, individual small-business owners sell their catch to processors large and small. The fishing economy supports an entire community, from shipyards to canneries to net shops. A recent report from the Alaska governor's office warns, "As a result of the glut of Chilean farm-raised salmon in the world market, volume-related price drops of Chilean fillets in the U.S. marketplace have preempted profitable and viable participation by Alaska salmon producers of consumer-ready fillets."

As consumers, it is important to understand the true cost of a $3.99-a-pound (or less) salmon fillet in a broad context. Buying wild salmon, or buying responsibly farmed salmon from a farm with a recognized certification of quality, might cost more, but is the only way to avoid contributing to the overwhelming environmental and economic impact caused by these agro-chemical fish farms.

It's important to note that not all farm-raised salmon is the same. Just as there are small growers bringing high-quality organic produce to market, there are boutique salmon farmers bringing high-quality farm-raised salmon to market. I visited one of them in June 2003. Gilpin Bradley, from Wester Ross Salmon, Ltd. in Ullapool, Scotland, is committed to high-quality salmon farming (see page 188). Bradley is a member of Scottish Quality Salmon (SQS), an organization that guarantees that salmon is farmed to the highest standards of fish welfare and environmental care. Farmed salmon from SQS members is tagged in the market with a Tartan Quality Mark, distinguishing it from other farmed salmon. France labels foods that have met their rigorous high-quality standards with a Label Rouge tag. SQS salmon was the first fish and first non-French product to obtain the prestigious Label Rouge in 1992.

Large multinational corporations control one-third of the aquaculture industry, driving down prices, overloading the net pens with fish, and in general not following practices safe for either the fish or the environment. However, a small percentage of salmon farmers are committed to producing high-quality salmon using environmentally safe practices. They are banding together as members of a quality assurance board and labeling their fish just as the SQS members do. It is our job as consumers to ask questions and, hopefully, to only buy fish that meets a high standard of excellence.

SALMON AND HEALTH

High-quality salmon is not only a delicious protein source but a valuable one, too. Salmon is rich in omega-3 fatty acids that help lower blood triglycerides and cholesterol levels, keeping the heart healthy. Salmon contains vitamins A, D, B_6, and B_{12}, as well as niacin and riboflavin. Salmon is also a good source of vitamin E, a powerful antioxidant. A French study has found that people who eat fish at least once a week are less likely to develop dementia. Other laboratory studies indicate that fish oils (particularly omega-3s) help control inflammatory processes that are associated with Alzheimer's.

Registered dietitians involved in what is called "nutritional therapy" are exploring the connections between what we eat and how we feel. Their research suggests that foods high in omega-3 fatty acids have mood-lifting powers. Salmon is a perfect source, along with enriched eggs and flaxseed oil. Eating foods high in omega-3s have also been reported to help fight wrinkles, making the skin look and feel younger—the equivalent of a nutritional face-lift.

Wow—all of these incredible nutrients packed into a piece of fish! Why then, with all the wonderful attributes of this "miracle fish," has there been a flurry of negative press? Because not all salmon is the same, nor is it all high quality. As with anything we eat, the more we learn and understand about how a food is grown or raised and comes to market, the smarter we are in our choices of what to eat, and this certainly applies to salmon. All the controversy surrounding contaminants found in salmon relates to farmed salmon—eating wild salmon has now been shown to be better for consumers' health.

A recent study in the journal *Science* confirmed the findings of three smaller studies on the safety of farmed salmon. This larger study analyzed the contaminants in two metric tons of salmon and found much higher levels of PCBs and several other contaminants in the tissue of farmed salmon than in wild salmon. It found more than a sevenfold difference in PCB levels, with farmed salmon having an average of 36.63 parts per billion and wild salmon having 4.75 ppb.

"The cancer risk associated with PCBs has been a point of contention for years. PCBs have not been proved to cause cancer in people, and industry workers who were exposed to higher levels did not have a higher cancer rate," says Dr. Michael Gallo of the Cancer Institute at the Robert Wood Johnson Medical School.

On the other hand, Dr. Linda Birnbaum, director of the experimental toxicology division at the Environmental Protection Agency says, "You can spend a lot of time arguing about the numbers and the exact details, but in some ways I think it's more useful just to look at the levels. They are so much higher in farmed salmon. That gives you an indication that maybe there's something there that you don't want." She adds, "Personally, I eat a fair amount of fish, but I try to limit my consumption of farmed fish."

As consumers, we have choices in the marketplace—organic produce vs. conventionally grown produce, free-range poultry vs. cooped-up birds, artisanal breads vs. factory-produced loaves—and now we have substantiated findings that alert us to the differences between farm-raised and wild salmon. Yes, wild salmon costs more. In fact, wild salmon can cost twice as much as farm-raised salmon and can skyrocket to $16 or more per pound for Copper River salmon. Personally, I'm willing to pay it. I can see the difference, I can taste the difference, and now I know that it makes a difference to my health. But as already mentioned, since the demand for salmon is such that wild salmon alone will not suffice, the support of discerning consumers for high-quality farmed salmon can help ensure that these farmers survive and thrive.

CATCHING, CLEANING, BUYING, STORING, AND PREPARING SALMON

As fresh as fresh gets, there is nothing like hooking a salmon, steelhead, or, for that matter, any good-eating fish, and then cooking it just hours later. The serenity of the wait, the thrill of the tug on the line, and the struggle to reel in the fish are exhilarating and addictive. I know, because I caught my first fish, a 75-pound halibut, this past May! Seasoned fishermen (of both genders) can skip over my description of going from catch to gutting because this is second nature to them, but for me this was a crucial learning step in preparing a fish for a meal. *And,* if you are going to fish, you've got to know how to clean and gut your catch. If you don't fish for salmon, skip the next paragraph and learn the tips for shopping for fish.

cleaning and gutting salmon

As soon as you pull the fish out of the water, strike it on the back of the head with a rock, hammer, or club. This usually renders the fish unconscious. With the stomach of the fish facing you, place a sharp knife in the anal opening just deep enough to cut through the flesh. Make a vertical cut all the way up from the anus to the operculum (the cover over the gills). Drain the blood and spread open the abdominal cavity. Reach in and remove all the innards, or entrails. Wash the cavity of the fish to free it of blood, being sure to get the blood out of the tissues. Cut off and discard the fins. If you prefer leaving the head on, immediately place the fish on ice. If you prefer removing the head, then place a knife right behind the gills on a slightly angled line perpendicular to the spinal column. Cut through on both sides, separating the head, with gills attached, from the body, and then place the fish on ice. (If you want to make Salmon Stock, page 77, rinse the head, remove the gills (see directions below), and place the salmon head on ice as well.)

shopping for salmon

Whether shopping for fish, vegetables, dairy, meat, or poultry, the key is to buy fresh, well-cared-for foods. In the best-case scenario, the goal is to buy locally and seasonally, to make the connection between the grower or producer and the consumer. Living in Portland, Oregon, I can do that—I can buy, in season, fresh Oregon-caught salmon from a fisherman at my local farmers' market. I know how lucky I am, but I also know that, in this global marketplace, Copper River salmon caught one day off the shores of Cordova, Alaska, can be shipped overnight to restaurants and high-end fish markets all over the United States and farther. I also know that farmed salmon raised in Chile, or Norway, or off the coast of Scotland can be shipped overnight to global markets. Here is how to use your senses to make sure that the fish you buy, wherever they are from, are fresh.

The first rule of shopping for fresh fish, whether you are shopping at a supermarket, tiny corner fish store, or a specialty market with a fish counter, is to get to know your fishmonger. If you are going to shop often for fish, introduce yourself, ask questions, become a regular. Find out when the shipment of fish arrived, whether it has been frozen (not necessarily a bad thing), and where it came from. I like to shop in markets where the fish are on ice in a refrigerated glass case, where the counters and cases look clean, and the fish are protected from direct sun, flies, and so on. I avoid, if at all possible, fish sold in prewrapped packages. And if I walk into a market that has a really strong, smelly fish odor, rather than smelling like the sea, I walk right out.

Now, look at an individual fish. Is it moist and glistening? Is the skin silvery and bright? Are the salmon's eyes protruding, bright, and clear? If the fish has been cut into fillets, do the fillets look moist and freshly cut rather than flat and browned at the edges? If the fish looks good visually and you pick out a fillet for the fishmonger to weigh, feel free to ask to smell it. Fresh fish doesn't smell; there is no fishy odor. Anyone selling top-quality fish should be delighted you asked. If you feel shy about asking, then just stand close to the scale as the counter clerk is weighing the fish and take a whiff. Touch is important, too. If you are buying a whole fish or even a whole side of salmon, ask to touch the skin. A gentle nudge with your fingertip will let you know whether the fish is resilient and firm rather than mushy. Also, ask to see the gills; they should be bright pink or red. If the gills are pale or brownish, the fish is old. Finally, if you do establish a "regular customer" relationship with your fishmonger and you're happy, be sure to give feedback: "The fillets of salmon I bought last week were terrific; I grilled them just the way you suggested." It's all about caring at every level in the chain of food processing and marketing.

Along with knowing how fresh the fish is, consumers rightfully want to know where the fish is from and how it was raised. Now, more than ever, we see little white signs stuck in the ice next to the fillets indicating the fish's origin, upbringing, and whether it is organic. However, the labels used to describe fish can be more than a little confusing, so a few words of clarification are in order.

ORGANIC Most salmon labeled "organic" is actually farmed salmon originating from the North Atlantic, off the coasts of Ireland, Nova Scotia, and Scotland. Europe has had organic certifying agencies in place for over five years. Salmon farms with organic certification must operate in adherence with a strict set of standards.

CERTIFIED ORGANIC You should not see any salmon, or for that matter any fish or seafood, labeled "certified organic." The U.S. Department of Agriculture (USDA), which governs organic rules in this country, has not yet set standards and rules for aquatic species. The USDA organic seal applies only to crops and animals raised on land that meet strict federal guidelines.

ALL-NATURAL, FARM-RAISED SALMON OR ENVIRONMENTALLY SUSTAINABLE SALMON This is unregulated marketing language that pertains to farmed salmon. As consumer concern for the environment and the quality of the fish continues to grow, smaller aquaculture businesses are responding and adopting environmentally friendly and responsible aquatic farming practices. Stocking densities are reduced, the feed is organic, the salmon are raised without the use of antibiotics, the pigment used in the feed is from a natural source, and the use of pesticides to treat sea lice is strongly restricted.

CONVENTIONALLY FARMED SALMON Typically, this is Atlantic salmon farm-raised by large multinational corporations using dense stocking practices, non-organic feed, antibiotics to maintain the health of the salmon, and pesticides to control disease. Almost always the least expensive of all salmon sold. Conventionally farmed salmon most often comes from Europe, British Columbia, Chile, and other coastal states in the U.S.

WILD SALMON This is salmon caught in their natal waters by commercial or tribal fishermen using either troll or gillnet fishing methods that are tightly regulated by state fishery management agencies.

WILD-CAUGHT SALMON A campaign to boost the image of Oregon salmon had to back off from the word "wild" because fish activists objected, as many of the salmon caught off the Oregon coast are in fact reared in hatcheries. These fish are now labeled wild-caught salmon. In Alaska, hatchery-reared salmon account for about 30 percent of the catch. In the lower 48 states, hatcheries account for over 50 percent of the salmon caught.

storing salmon

What any fisherman worth his salt will tell you is that keeping freshly caught fish clean, iced, and quickly processed is critical to quality and, of course, safety from spoilage. Ideally, buy fish on the day you plan to eat it. If you must store fish for a day, or two at the most, then store it carefully wrapped in the coldest part of the refrigerator. If the fish is enclosed in butcher paper, place it in a lock-top plastic bag or rewrap it tightly in plastic wrap. (Salmon fillets and steaks will get water spotted if directly in contact with water or ice.) Fill a deep pan or bowl with ice or, better yet, reusable gel ice packs, and place the wrapped fish on top. Store it on the bottom shelf or the back of a lower shelf in the refrigerator. (If using ice, drain off the melted water and add more ice as needed.)

freezing salmon

You must take special precautions to freeze salmon successfully. How you wrap your fish and at what temperature you store it is critical. For the last five years, I have had the opportunity to buy Copper River salmon air-shipped straight from Copper River Seafoods in Cordova, Alaska (see Sources, page 188). I purchase 50 pounds each season and have the processor cut the salmon into whole sides or 1-pound fillets and vacuum-seal the packages. The salmon is flash-frozen and air-shipped to me frozen. I have a manual-defrosting freezer that keeps the fish just below 0°F. The fish keeps beautifully for six months. (Manual-defrosting freezers are better than self-defrosting ones, because the process of self-defrosting dries out frozen foods more quickly.)

Vacuum-sealed packaging is ideal. If you fish, or have generous friends who fish, or are able to purchase high-quality salmon in season and want to freeze it, think about either purchasing a small vacuum-sealer or making friends with a butcher or fishmonger and paying them to vacuum-seal the fish for you. Otherwise, wrap the fish as tightly as possible (without air pockets) in several thicknesses of plastic wrap, place it in a lock-top freezer bag, squeeze out the air in the bag, and freeze the fish. If you have a chest freezer or upright freezer that will keep the fish below 0°F, the salmon should be fine for up to six months. If you are storing the salmon in the freezer compartment of a refrigerator, plan to use it within one month.

thawing salmon

The best way to thaw salmon is to place the unopened package of salmon in a bowl or pan in the refrigerator. Fillets or a side of salmon usually thaw overnight, depending on the thickness of the fish. Thawing fish at room temperature can lead to bacterial growth because the outside of the fish is getting warm and beginning to spoil while the center is still frozen. If you need to thaw fish quickly, submerge the package in a bowl of cool water until thawed. Depending on the amount of fish you are thawing, this could take 1 to 2 hours. Use thawed fish sooner rather than later, within 24 hours.

basic preparation techniques

Though specific preparation directions are given in each recipe, the basics, such as scaling, removing the gills, filleting, skinning, removing pin bones, and skin-drying salmon are detailed here. A fishmonger will usually do some of these basics for you, if you ask. As a courtesy, I prefer to call in advance and place an order. This way, the fishmonger has time to prepare my fish without rushing if I happen to walk in at a busy time.

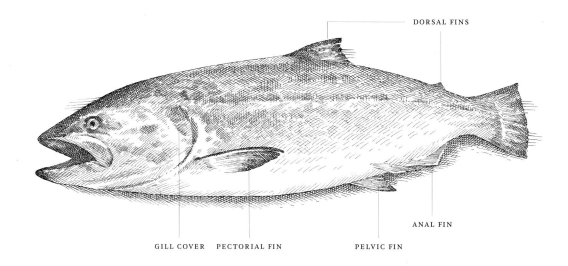

DORSAL FINS

ANAL FIN

GILL COVER   PECTORIAL FIN

PELVIC FIN

SCALING All the recipes in this book specify in the ingredient list whether the salmon needs to be scaled or not. Scaling salmon is necessary if you are planning to cook a whole fish, or fillets or steaks with the skin on. This is a messy job, and, honestly, one of my least favorites, so if you are buying fish that needs to be scaled ask the fishmonger to do this for you. To do it yourself: If working with a whole fish, place the fish in the sink on top of several layers of newspaper spread out wide. You can also place the fish in a very large plastic bag to contain the scales as they come flying off. Using kitchen shears, cut off the three fins on the underbelly, then turn the fish over and remove the dorsal fins if they are still attached. Using a fish scaler (available at cookware stores) or the back of a stiff knife (I use a small chef's knife), scrape the skin from the tail towards the head. Run your hands over the fish to feel for any scales you've missed. Rinse off the fish and pat dry with paper towels.

REMOVING THE GILLS Salmon breathe through their gills, feathery tissues that allow the fish to extract oxygen from the water in exchange for carbon dioxide. The gills need to be removed if you are cooking a whole salmon, or using the head to make Salmon Stock (page 77), because they contain impurities and will make a sauce or stock taste bitter. Lift up the gill plate, the flap just behind the eyes, on one side of the head and you'll see the gills—feathery tissue that is pink or red and half-moon shaped. They are attached at the head and at the collarbone. Using sharp kitchen shears or a knife, cut out the gills on one side of the head at the two attached points. Turn the fish over and repeat to remove the gills from the other side. Discard the gills, rinse the fish, and pat it dry with paper towels.

FILLETING If you are purchasing a whole salmon and are planning to fillet it, ask the fish market to fillet it for you. It takes a little practice to get clean, smooth fillets off the bones without jagged cuts. But, if you want to fillet your own, here is the method I use. Assuming the salmon has already been cleaned through the belly (see "Cleaning and Gutting Salmon," page 26), place the salmon on its side and make a diagonal cut just behind the gill cover. Do this on both sides, and then cut through to detach the head. Using a sharp, flexible boning knife, slice down the length of the fish, starting at the head end, making a cut all the way through the spine bone. Again starting at the head end and working your way down to the tail while keeping your knife almost flat against the bones, skim the knife along the bones in a smooth sliding motion, trying not to stop. As you are slicing, lift the fillet with your other hand, allowing you to see the flesh being sliced away from the bone. Slice in this manner all the way down to the tail. Turn the salmon over and repeat the process on the other side to remove the second fillet. Trim off the rib bones from the upper side of each fillet. If desired, save the head, bones, and trimmings for making Salmon Stock (page 77).

SKINNING A SALMON FILLET   Lay the salmon fillet skin side down with the tail facing you. Grip the tail with a piece of paper towel, or you can put a little coarse salt on your fingertips to create traction. Using a sharp, flexible boning knife, angle the blade towards the skin and, while you are gripping the tail skin with one hand, cut along the skin as smoothly as you can. Cut all the way from the tail to the head end, keeping the skin taut. Discard the skin.

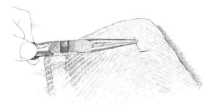

REMOVING PIN BONES   Run your fingertips along the flesh side of the fillet until you feel the pin bones. Using either clean needle–nose pliers (I keep a pair in the kitchen precisely for this use) or fish tweezers, grasp the end of each bone and pull it straight out and away from the flesh to remove it. If you try to pull them upwards or backwards it tends to tear the flesh.

CUTTING FILLETS   Most of the main–course recipes in this book call for a 6–ounce fillet as a portion size. Though restaurants sometimes serve as much as 8 ounces of salmon on an entrée plate, I think that is an unnecessarily large serving. In addition, most of the recipes call for the salmon to be cut into fillet portions rather than into steaks. Salmon steaks, unless they are cut from the tail end, are tricky to cook because the belly flaps (the thin pieces at the ends of the steaks) hang down and cook more quickly than the center of the steak. Salmon steaks can be deboned and tied into medallions, but this is a fussy and time-consuming job.

There are several ways to cut salmon fillets from a boned side of salmon: Place a whole fillet skin side up and cut the fillet crosswise into straight-sided portions. Or, cut the fillet in half lengthwise, and then cut crosswise into portions. If you want to serve only the thicker portions, reserve the belly portion of the fillet for chowder or for tartare. For diagonally sliced fillets, start at the head end, following the natural diagonal line of the fillet. Cut fillet portions on a sharp angle through the flesh. If you look at the cross section, it will not be a rectangular shaped piece, but a parallelogram with angled sides. As you cut portions, the pieces at the head end should be thinner in width than at the tail end in order to achieve the same weight per serving. Finally, to achieve a butterfly cut from a skinless square-cut portion of salmon, cut straight down the middle of the flesh, but not all the way through. Fold back the two halves as if the piece of salmon were a butterfly opening its wings. The piece of salmon will now look like a salmon steak without the bone in the center. Make a slightly deeper cut if the butterflied portion does not lie flat.

SKIN-DRYING SALMON   I learned about this technique for achieving crisp-skinned salmon several years ago from an article by Thomas Keller (owner of the famed French Laundry restaurant in Yountville, California) in the *Los Angeles Times* food section. He writes, "The skin of many fish is exquisite, never more so than when it's crisped to a delicate wafer-thin crunch accompanying the sweet, soft flesh. Crisp fish skin should taste clean and fresh, with the concentrated flavor of the fish itself. Its colors and design are vivid on the plate. The fork clicks on its surface. It cracks brittlely beneath a knife."

The critical technique is to remove as much water as possible from the skin of the fish before cooking it. Keller writes: "Remove some of that water mechanically, by drawing a knife blade firmly back and forth over the fish, the way a wiper blade moves across a windshield. The pressure compresses the skin and squeezes the water to the surface, and the knife blade carries it away. Repeat this until no more water rises to the surface." Periodically wipe the knife blade clean with a paper towel to remove what looks like grayish scum.

APPETIZERS

Salmon Tartare

Suggested wine: Champagne; domestic sparkling wine; Chablis; Austrian grüner veltliner

Serve salmon tartare as an elegant appetizer or first course. Have the tartare take center stage on an oversized plate with an artful flourish of paper-thin cucumber slices strewn about. A drizzle of extra-virgin olive oil, a scattering of minced chives, and a dusting of fleur de sel make this a showstopper for a sophisticated dinner party, perfect for a New Year's Eve party.

Buy your salmon from a reputable fishmonger, making sure it is very fresh. In fact, the best kind of salmon to use for curing or eating raw is salmon that has been flash-frozen at sea. The freshly caught salmon is put on ice immediately and then sold to a "floating processor" vessel at sea, where the fish is gutted and flash-frozen. Any parasites in the flesh of the fish are killed when the fish is frozen just below 0°F for seven days.

SERVES 6 AS AN APPETIZER

1 center-cut salmon fillet (8 ounces), skin and pin bones removed *(see page 32)*

1 tablespoon minced fresh chives, plus more for garnish

1 tablespoon minced shallots

1 tablespoon minced fresh flat-leaf parsley

1½ teaspoons fresh lemon juice

1 tablespoon extra-virgin olive oil, plus more for drizzling

¾ teaspoon kosher or sea salt

Pinch or 2 of freshly ground white pepper

1 English cucumber

Fleur de sel for sprinkling *(see Cook's Note)*

Using a very sharp knife, cut the salmon into ¼-inch dice. (Do not use a food processor, as it damages the texture of the fish, making it coarse and mushy.) Place the salmon in a medium bowl. Gently fold in the 1 tablespoon chives, the shallots, parsley, and lemon juice. Stir in the 1 tablespoon olive oil and add the salt and pepper. Cover and refrigerate for at least 30 minutes or up to 8 hours. Remove from the refrigerator 20 minutes before serving.

Cut the cucumber in half crosswise. Cut each half into long, paper-thin slices. Set aside on a plate, covered, until ready to serve.

To assemble, using 6 large salad or dinner plates, scatter several slices of cucumber around each plate in a random, artful way. Leave the center of each plate open. Spoon approximately $\frac{1}{4}$ cup tartare into a mound in the center of each plate. Drizzle olive oil over the cucumber slices, garnish with chives, and sprinkle with a bit of fleur de sel. Serve immediately.

COOK'S NOTE

Fleur de sel is an aromatic salt that has been evaporated from seawater. It has large flaky crystals and a pure briny flavor and aroma. I buy either fleur de sel from France's Brittany coast or from the Camargue region near Provence.

Gravlax

Suggested wine: Chablis; pinot gris; sauvignon blanc

One of the most delicate and least-embellished salmon preparations is gravlax, a Scandinavian specialty in which the fish is cured by means of a salt and sugar rub. No cooking is involved. I like to think of this paper-thin sliced raw fish as one step beyond Japanese sashimi. Typically, gravlax is seasoned with fresh dill, a brandy such as Cognac, and spruce sprigs. Not everyone has a spruce tree growing in his or her yard, including me, so I've decided to re-create that woodsy flavor by including gin in my recipe. The gin's mild juniper berry flavor is a lovely accent with the dill. Serve the salmon with buttered pumpernickel as an appetizer or first course along with thin slices of cucumber. The salmon can be garnished with chopped chives, scallions, capers, minced shallots, or lemon zest. Drizzle the salmon with extra-virgin olive oil if you desire.

SERVES 10 AS A FIRST COURSE OR 20 AS AN APPETIZER

½ cup coarse sea salt or kosher salt
½ cup sugar
1 salmon fillet (3 to 4 pounds), skin on and scaled, pin bones removed *(see page 32)*
10 sprigs fresh dill, coarsely chopped
¼ cup gin

Select a 2-inch-deep glass or ceramic baking dish that fits the length of the fish as closely as possible. In a small bowl, combine the salt and sugar and spread half of this mixture on the bottom of the baking dish. Lay the salmon, skin side down, in the dish. Gently rub the remaining salt mixture over the flesh side of the fillet. Spread the dill over the fillet. Slowly drizzle the gin over the fish, being careful not to rinse off the salt cure.

Place a large sheet of plastic wrap directly on top of the fish. Select a slightly smaller baking dish, or some other large, flat object, to rest on top of the fish. Place something that weighs several pounds in the top of the dish. I use full beer bottles set on their sides. Place the weighted salmon in the refrigerator for at least 2 days or up to 5 days. Turn the salmon once a day, being sure to weight the salmon after each turn.

To serve, skin the fillet, then cut the fillet into ⅛-inch-thick crosswise slices. Arrange on a platter and garnish as desired. Gravlax keeps for up to 1 week in the refrigerator. To freeze for up to 3 months, wrap the gravlax completely in plastic wrap and then in a double layer of aluminum foil.

Smoked Salmon Pillows

Suggested wine: Oregon pinot noir; French chardonnay such as St. Verán or Mâconnais

These hors d'oeuvres are adorable, like fluffy little square pillows! Nothing beats these easy-to-make and fabulous-tasting puff pastry appetizers, crisp and warm from the oven. The smoked salmon filling is a snap to make, and with such a small quantity to mix, I prefer to blend it by hand with a rubber spatula rather than have to wash my food processor. Keep a batch in the freezer for spur-of-the-moment entertaining or a stress-free cocktail party. Smoked salmon pillows and Champagne make a perfect pairing.

MAKES 36 PILLOWS; SERVES 12 AS AN APPETIZER

1 package (17.3 ounces) frozen puff pastry sheets
4 ounces goat cheese, at room temperature
4 ounces smoked salmon (lox), finely diced
3 tablespoons snipped fresh chives
1 tablespoon heavy (whipping) cream
1 large egg, lightly beaten
All-purpose flour for dusting

Thaw the puff pastry at room temperature for 30 minutes. While the pastry is thawing, prepare the filling: In a small bowl, combine the goat cheese, salmon, chives, cream, and 1 tablespoon of the beaten egg. Reserve the remaining egg for glazing the top of the pastry. Cover and refrigerate while rolling out the pastry.

Unfold one of the pastry sheets and place it on a work surface lightly dusted with flour. Using a rolling pin, roll out the pastry into a 12-inch square. Trim the edges, preferably with a pastry cutter or pizza wheel, to form an exact square. Slide the pastry sheet onto a baking sheet, cover it with plastic wrap, and refrigerate the pastry while you roll out the second sheet. Dust the work surface with additional flour, if needed, and roll out and cut the second pastry sheet exactly like the first one.

Using a ruler and a paring knife, measure and lightly score the second pastry, marking off six 2-inch-wide columns and six 2-inch-wide rows, forming thirty-six 2-inch squares. Do not cut through the pastry; just score it lightly enough to see the lines. Remove the filling from the refrigerator and place 1 rounded teaspoon of filling in the center of each square.

Remove the pastry sheet from the refrigerator and, lifting carefully, place it on top of the first pastry sheet. Align the sides exactly. Using a chopstick or the back of a table knife, lightly press down between the rows and columns to form little ravioli or pillows. Press just enough to see the mounds of filling. Using a pastry brush, brush the top of the pastry completely with some of the remaining beaten egg. Using a pizza cutter or pastry wheel, cut the pastry along the indented lines into 2-inch squares. Press lightly along the edges to seal the filling inside. Arrange the squares 1 inch apart on 2 nonstick or parchment-lined baking sheets. Cover with plastic wrap and refrigerate for at least 20 minutes or up to 1 day. (The pillows can be made up to this point and frozen for up to 1 month. Once the pastry is cold, arrange them in a single layer between sheets of waxed paper in a covered freezer container.)

Position the oven racks in the center and top third of the oven. Preheat the oven to 425°F. Bake the pastries, rotating the pans halfway through the baking time, until crisp, puffed, and golden, about 12 minutes. Let cool on the pans for 5 minutes. Use a spatula to carefully lift and transfer the pillows to a warmed platter. Serve immediately.

Grilled Smoked Salmon Sandwiches

Suggested wine: Alsatian pinot gris; Champagne; domestic sparkling wine

There is nothing more playful than serving your guests miniature grilled sandwiches as an hors d'oeuvre—especially when they are filled with luscious smoked salmon and a dill-and-lemon-infused cream cheese. A snap to make, the sandwiches can be assembled ahead of time, ready to grill. They are best served hot: crisp, creamy, and salmon-packed.

MAKES 16 WEDGES; SERVES 8 AS AN APPETIZER

3 ounces cream cheese, at room temperature

1 tablespoon crème fraîche or sour cream

2 teaspoons chopped fresh dill

1 teaspoon grated lemon zest

⅛ teaspoon freshly ground pepper

⅛ teaspoon kosher or sea salt

8 slices firm white bread, preferably Pepperidge Farm or Oroweat, crusts removed

5 ounces thinly sliced smoked salmon (lox)

4 tablespoons (½ stick) unsalted butter, at room temperature

In a small bowl, mix together the cream cheese, crème fraîche or sour cream, dill, lemon zest, pepper, and salt.

Arrange 4 bread slices on a work surface. Spread each bread slice with 1 heaping tablespoon of the cheese mixture. Divide the salmon among the 4 bread slices, placing it on top of the cheese mixture. Top each with a slice of the remaining bread. Using half of the butter, spread the top side of each sandwich with butter.

Heat a griddle or a large sauté pan, preferably nonstick, over medium-high heat. Add as many sandwiches as will fit the pan without crowding, buttered side down, and cook until browned on the bottom, 2 to 3 minutes. While the sandwiches are cooking on the first side, spread the remaining butter over the top of the bread. Turn the sandwiches over. Cook until nicely brown on the second side, 2 to 3 minutes. Transfer to a cutting board.

Using a serrated knife, cut each sandwich in half on the diagonal, then each half on the diagonal again to form 4 triangles. Arrange on a warmed plate and serve immediately. (The sandwiches can be assembled up to 2 hours in advance; cover and refrigerate until ready to grill.)

Smoked Salmon with Lemon–Chive Shortbreads

Suggested wine: riesling; pinot grigio

These may seem like fussy little appetizers, but they're not. What I like to do is make the dough, roll out and cut the shortbreads, then freeze the unbaked cookies. In a pinch, when company is coming, I'll put a couple dozen on a baking sheet straight from the freezer and have instant hors d'oeuvres. The herbed cream cheese is a snap to mix together, or you can buy a good-quality herbed blend from the local deli where you buy lox. This recipe makes plenty for a large cocktail party, or you can pull out a dozen or so at a time for a dinner party.

MAKES ABOUT 60 SHORTBREADS; SERVES 20 AS AN APPETIZER

Lemon-Chive Shortbreads

1 cup all-purpose flour

3 tablespoons medium-grind cornmeal

½ teaspoon kosher or sea salt

2 tablespoons finely snipped fresh chives

Grated zest of 1 lemon

½ cup (1 stick) unsalted butter, softened 30 minutes at room temperature,
   cut into small cubes

4 ounces goat cheese, crumbled

4 ounces cream cheese, at room temperature

¾ teaspoon freshly ground pepper

2 teaspoons minced fresh dill, plus more for garnish

10 ounces thinly sliced smoked salmon (lox)

All-purpose flour for dusting

In a food processor fitted with the metal blade, combine the flour, cornmeal, and salt. Pulse several times to combine. Add the chives and lemon zest and pulse twice to combine. Distribute the butter and goat cheese evenly over the flour mixture. Pulse just until the dough forms a ball. Transfer the dough to a piece of plastic wrap, flatten into a disk, wrap well, and refrigerate for at least 1 hour before rolling.

Meanwhile, in a small bowl, blend together the cream cheese, pepper, and the 2 teaspoons dill. Cover and refrigerate. Cut the salmon slices into 1-by-1$^{1}/_{2}$-inch strips. Roll the strips into little tubes and arrange on a plate ready to assemble the appetizers. Cover and refrigerate.

Position the oven racks in the center and lower third of the oven. Preheat the oven to 350°F. Have ready 2 nonstick or parchment-lined rimmed baking sheets. On a lightly floured work surface, using a rolling pin lightly dusted with flour, roll the dough $^{1}/_{8}$ inch thick. Cut out short-breads with a 1$^{1}/_{4}$-inch-diameter cookie cutter and place $^{1}/_{2}$ inch apart on the baking sheets. Gather the unused pieces of dough, reroll, and cut additional shortbreads until all the dough is used. Bake until lightly browned, 20 to 25 minutes. Let cool on wire racks.

To assemble, using a table knife, dab a small amount of the herbed cream cheese in the center of each of the shortbreads. Place a piece of salmon on top and garnish with a tiny sprig of dill. Arrange on a serving platter. Serve immediately, or loosely cover and keep at room temperature for up to 1 hour.

COOK'S NOTE

These shortbreads are best when baked the day of serving. They freeze well unbaked. Roll and cut out the cookies, layer between sheets of waxed paper, and freeze in a covered container. The shortbreads can be made up to 1 month in advance. Bake without thawing, allowing for a slightly longer baking time. Alternatively, the dough can be made 2 days in advance, wrapped tightly, and refrigerated.

Salmon Rillettes

Suggested wine: California or French chardonnay; chardonnay–semillon blend

I obtained this recipe years ago from Lucien Vanel, who owns Restaurant Vanel in the old city of Toulouse, France. The mixture improves with age, making it a perfect do-ahead hors d'oeuvre for a party. It will keep up to 1 week under a layer of clarified butter. Plan to make it at least 2 days before serving to allow the flavors to meld.

SERVES 12 AS AN APPETIZER

1 salmon fillet (1 pound), skin and pin bones removed
¼ teaspoon kosher or sea salt
1 cup (2 sticks) unsalted butter, at room temperature
1 large shallot, minced
2 tablespoons dry white wine
4 ounces smoked salmon (lox), cut into ¼-inch dice
2 tablespoons olive oil
1 tablespoon fresh lemon juice
1 large egg yolk
Pinch freshly grated nutmeg
Freshly ground white pepper

Cut the fillet into 4 equal portions. Sprinkle with the salt and let stand at room temperature for 20 minutes.

To make clarified butter for sealing the rillettes, melt 7 tablespoons of the butter in a medium sauté pan. Pour the butter into a 1-cup glass measure and set aside until the foam comes to the top and the milky residue settles to the bottom. Skim off the foam and carefully pour the clear yellow liquid into another measuring cup or small bowl. Discard the milky residue. Set the clarified butter aside.

Using the same sauté pan set over medium heat, melt 2 tablespoons of the butter until it foams. Add the shallot and sauté until soft but not browned, about 2 minutes. Add the salted salmon pieces in one layer and pour the wine over the top. Cover the salmon with a piece of waxed paper, and then with a tight-fitting lid. Cook for 2 minutes. Turn the salmon, cover, and cook just until the fish turns opaque, about 2 minutes longer. Remove the pan from the heat but keep it covered and let the salmon cool in the pan.

In a food processor fitted with the metal blade, process the remaining 7 tablespoons butter until creamy. Use a fork to flake the cooled salmon and add it to the work bowl. Add the smoked salmon and pulse the mixture just until combined. The texture should be grainy—do not process until smooth. Add the olive oil, lemon juice, egg yolk, nutmeg, and a little pepper. Pulse just until combined. Taste and adjust the seasoning.

Pack the rillettes into either two 1-cup crocks or ramekins, or one 2-cup ramekin. Smooth the surface. If the clarified butter has solidified, heat it just until melted but not hot. Pour just enough butter over each ramekin to cover the rillettes by about $\frac{1}{3}$ inch. Refrigerate.

Remove from the refrigerator about 40 minutes before serving. Remove the layer of butter by running a paring knife around the rim of the ramekin and lifting off the butter. (Scrape any of the salmon mixture off the butter and save the butter for later cooking. Use within a couple of days.) Serve the rillettes at room temperature, accompanied with crostini or crackers.

Alder–Smoked Salmon Dip

Suggested wine: Alsatian or Oregon pinot gris

The salmon used in this recipe is hot–smoked salmon, often labeled "alder–smoked." Delicious and readily available, this salmon has a firmer texture and more pronounced flavor than cured or cold–smoked salmon such as lox. Don't substitute lox; the texture of the pâté would be completely different.

MAKES ABOUT 2 CUPS, SERVES 8 TO 10 AS AN APPETIZER

1 pound alder-smoked salmon, skin and pin bones removed
6 tablespoons (¾ stick) unsalted butter, at room temperature
½ cup finely diced celery
3 tablespoons capers, rinsed and drained
2 tablespoons minced fresh dill
3 tablespoons fresh lemon juice
½ teaspoon freshly ground pepper
¼ teaspoon kosher salt

Place the salmon in a large bowl and use a fork to flake it into very fine shreds. Add the butter and, using the fork, work the butter into the salmon until well blended. Add the celery, capers, dill, lemon juice, pepper, and salt. Mix gently to combine. Taste and adjust the seasoning. Transfer to a serving bowl. Serve immediately.

COOK'S NOTES

Serve this dip with crostini, pita chips, bagel chips, or lavosh. • This dip can be prepared up to 2 days in advance. Cover and refrigerate. Remove from the refrigerator 20 minutes before serving.

Salmon and Crisp Salmon-Skin Hand Rolls

Suggested wine: sauvignon blanc

I'm a huge fan of sushi and hand rolls. One of my favorite sushi bars in Portland, Murata, makes a fabulous, crisp salmon-skin hand roll. I've sat at the sushi bar and watched and ordered and eaten these enough times to figure out what is inside. I think I've come mighty close to duplicating their hand rolls. The recipe looks long because I've tried to include detailed instructions, but, actually, they are quite easy to make. One of my favorite things to do for casual entertaining is to have all the ingredients ready to assemble and then give a mini-class and let my guests roll their own hand rolls.

MAKES 8 HAND ROLLS; SERVES 4 TO 8 AS AN APPETIZER

1 cup short-grain Japanese sushi rice

1½ cups water

¼ cup mirin *(see Cook's Notes, page 51)*

2 tablespoons seasoned rice vinegar

1 salmon fillet (6 ounces) from the tail end, skin and pin bones removed *(see page 32)*, skin reserved

2½ tablespoons kecap manis *(see Cook's Notes, page 51)*

4 sheets toasted nori (7¼ by 8 inches)

1 tablespoon wasabi powder mixed with 1 tablespoon mirin

Sixteen (4-inch-long) fresh chive stems

1 small cucumber, peeled, halved lengthwise, seeded, and cut into thin strips about 4 inches long

16 sprigs fresh cilantro

Soy sauce for dipping

Place the rice in a bowl and cover with cold water. Swish the rice, washing it in several changes of cold water until the water runs clear. This removes the residual starch. Drain in a sieve. Place the rice in a heavy 2-quart saucepan and add the water. Cover the pan and bring the water to a boil over high heat, about 5 minutes. Reduce the heat to low and cook the rice at a bare simmer

CONTINUED

for 15 minutes. As tempting as it might be, don't remove the lid and peek at any point, or all the steam will escape. Remove from the heat and let stand for 15 minutes. (Alternatively, use a rice cooker and follow the manufacturer's instructions.)

Meanwhile, combine the mirin and rice vinegar in a heatproof, glass measuring cup. Microwave on high until warm, about 20 seconds. Otherwise, place the cup in a small pan of simmering water and heat until warm. Transfer the rice to a large shallow bowl. Using a wood or rubber spatula, drizzle half the mirin mixture over the rice and gently fold it in using a light lifting and folding motion to avoid mashing the rice. As you are doing this, fan the rice with a rolled-up section of newspaper. Add the remaining mirin mixture and continue folding and fanning to cool the rice, about 5 minutes total. The rice should glisten. Cover the rice with a clean, damp dish towel and set aside until ready to make the hand rolls. The prepared rice can be made several hours ahead and left standing at room temperature.

To prepare the salmon, set an oven rack or broiler pan about 4 inches from the broiler and pre-heat the broiler. Cut the salmon into 8 long strips and brush each strip with some of the kecap manis. Arrange on a rimmed baking sheet lined with aluminum foil. Cut the salmon skin into 8 long strips and brush each strip with some of the kecap manis. Arrange on the baking sheet. Broil the salmon and salmon skin until the skin begins to crackle and the salmon is bronzed, 3 minutes. Use a spatula or tongs to transfer the salmon to a plate. Turn the salmon skin over and broil until the skin is crackly and crisp, 2 to 3 minutes longer. Transfer to a plate and set aside.

To assemble the hand rolls, cut each piece of nori in half lengthwise to form eight $7\frac{1}{4}$-by-4-inch rectangles. Have ready a small bowl with lukewarm water and a clean, dry linen towel. Working with one piece of nori at a time, arrange a sheet vertically, shiny side down, on the towel. Dampen your fingertips lightly. Spread about $\frac{1}{3}$ cup rice on the lower half of the nori, patting it down lightly. Dampen your fingertips a bit more if the rice is sticking to your fingers. Use your finger or the back of a teaspoon to smear a diagonal line of wasabi paste across the rice. Stacking them together, place 1 piece salmon, 1 piece salmon skin, 2 chive stems, 2 to 3 strips cucumber, and 2 sprigs cilantro across the rice from the upper left corner to the bottom right.

To roll the nori, fold the lower left-hand corner of the nori over the filling towards the right side. Keep rolling the nori, now rolling over towards the left side to form a cone. Just before you get to the end, moisten your finger with a little water and moisten the top end of the nori to seal the edge of the cone. Place on a serving tray. Repeat to form 8 hand rolls. With a little practice, you'll be able to assemble 2 at a time. Serve immediately, with little bowls of soy sauce for dipping. (The hand rolls can be made up to 2 hours ahead. Arrange on a serving platter and cover tightly with plastic wrap to keep them from drying out.)

COOK'S NOTES

Mirin is a Japanese sweet rice wine. Made from glutinous rice, mirin is low in alcohol, sweet, and light golden in color. It is used in sauces, glazes, and, of course, to flavor sushi rice. Mirin is sold in bottles and is available in the Asian section of supermarkets or at Japanese grocery stores. Store in the refrigerator once opened. • Kecap manis is an Indonesian sweet soy sauce flavored with palm sugar, garlic, star anise, and other spices. It is sweeter, more complex, and thicker than soy sauce. It is used as a marinade, glaze, and condiment in Indonesian dishes. Kecap manis is sold in bottles and is available in Asian grocery stores or, occasionally, in well-stocked supermarkets with a large Asian clientele. Store in a cool, dry place once opened.

Vietnamese Salad Rolls with Salmon, Rice Vermicelli, Pea Shoots, and Hoisin

Suggested wine: gewürztraminer; riesling

Think of these as a salad you can hold in your hand. Flavorful, healthful, and beautiful to look at, these salad rolls make perfect hors d'oeuvres, a first course to the start of an Asian meal, or picnic fare for a summer outing. Even though the ingredient list is long, these are quick to put together and easy to assemble. My teenage daughter, Molly, makes these when I have left–over grilled salmon in the refrigerator. She uses whatever interesting greens I have on hand—watercress, mesclun, a little mint—and then pulls some bottled peanut sauce from the pantry shelf. Make this dipping sauce—it's terrific—but if you are in a hurry, bottled peanut sauce will work, too.

MAKES 8 SALAD ROLLS; SERVES 8 AS AN APPETIZER

Hoisin-Peanut Dipping Sauce

2 tablespoons chunky natural peanut butter, warmed slightly to soften

¼ cup hoisin sauce

¼ cup water

1 tablespoon Thai fish sauce *(nam pla)*

¾ teaspoon peeled and minced fresh ginger

¼ teaspoon red pepper flakes

2 tablespoons soy sauce

1 tablespoon fresh lemon juice

2 teaspoons peeled and minced fresh ginger

1 teaspoon honey

1 salmon fillet (12 ounces), pin bones removed *(see page 32)*

1 package (2 ounces) rice vermicelli (bean threads) *(see Cook's Notes)*

Eight (8- to 9-inch) round rice paper wrappers *(see Cook's Notes)*

2 ounces pea shoots *(see Cook's Notes)*

4 green onions, trimmed, halved lengthwise, and then cut into 4-inch lengths

16 sprigs fresh cilantro

TO MAKE THE DIPPING SAUCE: Combine the peanut butter, hoisin, water, fish sauce, ginger, and red pepper flakes in a small bowl. Stir until well blended. Cover and set aside until ready to serve.

In a small bowl, combine the soy sauce, lemon juice, ginger, and honey. Place the salmon in a shallow baking dish and pour the marinade over the top. Turn the salmon several times until it is well coated with the marinade and then set aside for 20 minutes.

Meanwhile, soak the rice vermicelli in a medium bowl of warm water until softened, about 20 minutes. Drain in a colander and set aside covered with a damp paper towel.

Set an oven rack or broiler pan about 4 inches from the broiler and preheat the broiler. Drain the marinade. Broil the salmon, skin side up, until bronzed, 3 minutes. Turn the salmon and broil until it is bronzed and flakes slightly when nudged with a fork, about 3 minutes. Remove and set aside to cool. When cool enough to handle, cut the salmon into 8 long, thin strips.

To assemble the salad rolls, have ready a large bowl of warm water and a clean, dry linen towel. Working with one rice paper wrapper at a time, dip the wrapper in the water for 5 seconds, turning to wet both sides. Arrange on the towel. As you assemble the rolls, use $^1/_8$ of the ingredients for each roll: Lay a small portion of pea shoots, horizontally, on the bottom third of the wrapper. Top with a small mound of noodles, spreading them horizontally. Place a piece of salmon, 2 pieces green onion, and 2 sprigs cilantro horizontally on top. Roll the wrapper over the filling, creating a cylinder. Roll it halfway over again and then fold in the sides of the cylinder, envelope style. Continue rolling the wrapper into a finished cylinder. Place on a platter and continue rolling the rest of the salad rolls. Cover with a damp paper towel and then with plastic wrap. Set aside at room temperature until ready to serve. The salad rolls can be made up to 2 hours ahead. When ready to serve, cut each salad roll in half on the diagonal. Arrange on a platter or on individual small plates and serve with little bowls of dipping sauce.

COOK'S NOTES

Rice vermicelli, also called bean threads or cellophane noodles, are translucent threads made from the starch of mung beans. They have a wonderful texture once softened. Typically, bean threads come in 2-ounce cellophane bags, usually bundled in packages of 6 or 8 and wrapped in neon pink or plastic mesh bags. • Rice paper wrappers (banh trang) *are sometimes labeled "spring roll wrappers." These are thin, translucent dried sheets made from rice, water, and salt. They come in various sizes and are either round or square. They are softened in warm water and used fresh, or they can be stuffed, rolled, and deep-fried. • Pea shoots* (dau miu) *are the delicate, crisp vines and tender leaves of the green pea plant. Pea shoots taste like a cross between peas and spinach, with a hint of spicy watercress. Look for these ingredients in well-stocked supermarkets or in Asian grocery stores.*

Salmon Cakes with Satsuma, Red Onion, and Jicama Slaw

Suggested wine: Spanish albariño or Portuguese alvarinho

What I love about this recipe is that, except for frying the salmon cakes, everything can be made ahead, and that takes the stress out of dinner parties. Just like perfect crab cakes that fall apart with the touch of a fork, these salmon cakes have no heavy binders and aren't bogged down with fillers such as bread crumbs. The fresh taste of salmon, accented with ginger, onion, and herbs, makes these light, delectable, and crisp edged when rolled in Japanese bread crumbs. As a nice contrast and an addition to the plate, I've added a citrus-infused jicama slaw with lots of cilantro, red onion, and plump satsuma oranges.

MAKES 12 SALMON CAKES; SERVES 6 AS AN APPETIZER

Salmon Cakes

1 salmon fillet (12 ounces), skin and pin bones removed *(see page 32)*

2 teaspoons olive oil

Kosher or sea salt

Freshly ground pepper

4 tablespoons (½ stick) unsalted butter

1 tablespoon peeled and minced fresh ginger

½ cup diced white onion

½ cup finely diced celery

½ cup finely diced red bell pepper

½ cup mayonnaise

1 tablespoon fresh lemon juice

¼ teaspoon cayenne pepper

1 teaspoon minced fresh thyme

2 teaspoons snipped fresh chives

2 tablespoons minced fresh flat-leaf parsley

CONTINUED

Salmon Cakes with Satsuma, Red Onion, and Jicama Slaw *continued*

Jicama Slaw

12 ounces jicama, peeled and cut into ⅛-by-2-inch matchsticks (about 2 cups)

½ small red onion, halved lengthwise and cut into thin wedges

3 satsuma oranges, peeled, white pith removed, and sectioned

⅓ cup chopped fresh cilantro

3 tablespoons extra-virgin olive oil

Juice of 1 lime

1 teaspoon Dijon mustard

¾ teaspoon ground cumin

¾ teaspoon kosher or sea salt

½ teaspoon sugar

Freshly ground pepper

1¼ cups panko (Japanese bread crumbs)

2 tablespoons vegetable oil

TO MAKE THE SALMON CAKES: Preheat the oven to 250°F. Place the salmon in a shallow baking dish, rub all over with the olive oil, and season lightly with salt and pepper to taste. Bake the fish until the fat between the layers turns opaque, almost white, and the fish flakes slightly when pierced with a knife, 20 to 25 minutes. Alternatively, insert an instant-read thermometer into the thickest part of the salmon; when it registers 125° to 130°F, the fish is done. Set aside to cool.

Meanwhile, in a nonstick skillet or sauté pan, melt 2 tablespoons of the butter over medium heat and swirl to coat the pan. Add the ginger, onion, celery, and bell pepper. Sauté, stirring frequently, until the vegetables are soft but not brown, about 4 minutes. Add ½ teaspoon of salt and a few grinds of pepper. Set aside to cool.

In a mixing bowl, combine the mayonnaise, lemon juice, cayenne pepper, thyme, chives, and parsley. Stir to blend. Using a fork, flake the salmon into small pieces and add it to the mixing bowl. Add the vegetables. Using a rubber spatula, gently mix the ingredients, being careful not to mash the salmon. Form the mixture into 12 cakes about 1¾ inches in diameter and ½ inch thick. Place the salmon cakes on a rimmed baking sheet, cover, and refrigerate for at least 40 minutes or up to 8 hours.

TO MAKE THE JICAMA SLAW: Combine the jicama, onion, satsumas, and cilantro in a large bowl. Toss to mix well. In a small bowl, combine the olive oil, lime juice, mustard, cumin, salt, sugar, and a few grinds of pepper to taste. Stir vigorously to blend. Taste and adjust the seasoning. Pour the dressing over all and toss to mix well. Taste and add more salt and pepper, if desired. Cover and refrigerate. (The jicama slaw can be made up to 1 day in advance.) Remove from the refrigerator 30 minutes before serving. Toss again just before serving.

To finish and fry the salmon cakes, spread the bread crumbs on a dinner plate and roll the salmon cakes in the bread crumbs, coating all sides well. Set aside. In a large sauté pan, preferably cast iron, heat the remaining 2 tablespoons butter and the oil over medium–high heat. Swirl to coat the pan. Working in batches and without crowding the pan, brown the salmon cakes on one side, about 3 minutes, then flip them over and brown the other side, about 3 minutes longer. Serve immediately, accompanied with the jicama slaw.

SOUPS

Spring Salmon and Sorrel Soup

Suggested wine: Austrian grüner veltliner; Oregon or Alsatian riesling; sauvignon blanc

Two of my favorite foods, wild salmon and sorrel, arrive in the market at about the same time in mid–May. Along with asparagus and strawberries, sorrel signals spring and a season of lighter fare, moving away from wintry stews to simple, freshly cooked dishes highlighting garden produce and fresh fish. Speckles of brilliant green dot this cream soup, thickened with potatoes and full of the tangy, lemony flavor that sorrel imparts. Served in a shallow bowl, a square of delicately pink roasted salmon sticks up in the center, surrounded by a pool of the luscious green–hued soup. Serve this as a light supper with a loaf of crusty bread or for brunch. Be on the lookout for sorrel, even ask your produce buyer to stock it, but if it isn't available, then fresh watercress is an acceptable substitute.

SERVES 4 AS A LIGHT SUPPER

5 cups Salmon Stock *(page 77)*

¾ pound red boiling potatoes, peeled and cut into small chunks

1 salmon fillet (about 10 ounces), skin and pin bones removed, cut into 4 equal portions, each about 2½ inches square

2 teaspoons olive oil

Kosher or sea salt

Freshly ground pepper

4 ounces sorrel leaves, stemmed, thick center ribs removed

3 tablespoons unsalted butter, at room temperature

1 cup heavy (whipping) cream

1½ tablespoons minced fresh flat-leaf parsley

Preheat the oven to 250°F. In a heavy soup pot, bring the stock to a boil. Add the potatoes. Lower the heat to a simmer, partially cover the pot, and cook the potatoes until tender when pierced with a knife, about 15 minutes.

CONTINUED

Meanwhile, arrange the salmon on a rimmed nonstick baking sheet or line a baking sheet with parchment paper. Rub the salmon with a little olive oil and sprinkle each piece lightly with salt and pepper to taste. Set aside. In a food processor fitted with the metal blade, purée the sorrel, pulsing on and off for about 30 seconds. Add the butter and process until the sorrel is completely puréed and blended with the butter. Transfer to a small bowl, cover, and set aside.

When the potatoes are tender, place the salmon in the oven and bake until the fat between the layers begins to turn white and the fish flakes slightly, 20 to 25 minutes. The fish will appear to be underdone because the color is so beautifully pink and vivid, but it should be fully cooked.

While the salmon is baking, finish the soup. Using an immersion blender, purée the soup directly in the soup pot. Alternatively, working in batches, purée the soup in a regular blender and then transfer the soup back to the pot. Add the cream and stir until the soup is barely simmering. Add the sorrel butter and stir until well combined. Add $1\frac{1}{2}$ teaspoons of salt and a few grinds of pepper. Taste and adjust the seasoning. Keep warm until the salmon is done.

To serve, ladle about $1\frac{1}{4}$ cups of soup into each of 4 warmed large, shallow soup or pasta bowls. Carefully place a piece of salmon in the center of each bowl and garnish with some minced parsley. Serve immediately.

COOK'S NOTE

This soup is best when made with salmon stock, but if you have neither the time nor the inclination to make the stock, substitute 5 cups of fish stock, often available frozen from your fishmonger. Another option is to use 4 cups low-sodium chicken broth and 1 cup water for the stock. Diluting the chicken broth with water gives the soup a less "chickeny" flavor, allowing the wonderful combination of sorrel and salmon to shine through.

Salmon, Leek, and Celery Root Chowder

Suggested wine: California or French chardonnay

Celery root, also called celeriac, is texturally close to potatoes when cooked and has a unique flavor reminiscent of celery and parsley. This brown, knobby vegetable is the root of a specially bred celery plant. Look for firm roots that are medium to large in size. Use a paring knife rather than a vegetable peeler to remove the rough peel.

SERVES 6 AS A LIGHT SUPPER

3 strips bacon, cut into ½-inch dice
3 leeks, white and light green part only, halved lengthwise and cut into ¼-inch-thick slices
1½ pounds celery root (celeriac), peeled, halved, and cut into ¼-inch-thick slices
3 cups bottled clam juice
1 bay leaf
3 sprigs fresh thyme
1 salmon fillet (12 ounces), skin and pin bones removed *(see page 32)*, cut into bite-sized pieces
1½ cups half-and-half
1 tablespoon chopped fresh tarragon
2 tablespoons chopped fresh flat-leaf parsley
2 teaspoons fresh lemon juice
Kosher or sea salt
Freshly ground pepper

In a heavy soup pot over medium–high heat, cook the bacon until crisp, about 5 minutes. Using a slotted spoon, transfer the bacon to a plate lined with paper towels to drain. Pour off all but 2 tablespoons of the fat from the pan. Add the leeks and sauté over medium–low heat, stirring frequently, until softened but not brown, about 5 minutes. Add the celery root, clam juice, bay leaf, and thyme. Bring to a boil. Reduce the heat to low, cover, and simmer until the celery root is tender, about 15 minutes.

Add the salmon, bacon, half–and–half, tarragon, and parsley to the soup pot. Cook just below a simmer until the salmon is cooked through, about 5 minutes. (The half–and–half will curdle if the soup comes to a boil.) Remove the bay leaf and sprigs of thyme. Add the lemon juice, and season to taste with salt and pepper. Stir gently to keep the salmon chunks intact. Serve immediately.

Spicy Corn Stew with Chunks of Salmon

Suggested wine: Spanish albariño or Portuguese alvarinho

This colorful meal-in-a-pot needs nothing more than a loaf of crusty bread to make a hearty supper. Add a salad if you like, but the stew is chock-full of vegetables. Making a corn broth from the cobs gives the soup an underlying complex sweet corn flavor. It's an ideal pairing with the salmon, and the addition of a poblano gives the stew a bright chile flavor without being overpoweringly hot. A squeeze of lime and a pungent kick of cilantro are the perfect garnish.

SERVES 6 AS A MAIN COURSE

6 fresh ears yellow corn, shucked

2 large sweet onions, such as Walla Walla, Vidalia, or Maui

2 tablespoons vegetable oil

8 cups cold water

3 tablespoons olive oil

2 celery stalks, cut into ½-inch dice

1 large poblano chile, seeded, deribbed, and cut into ½-inch dice *(see Cook's Note, page 66)*

1 tablespoon minced fresh thyme

2 cups heavy (whipping) cream

1 teaspoon kosher or sea salt

⅛ teaspoon cayenne pepper

1 salmon fillet (12 ounces), skin and pin bones removed *(see page 32)*, cut into bite-sized pieces

¼ cup packed fresh cilantro leaves

1 lime, cut into 6 wedges

Working with one ear of corn at a time, stand it upright, stem end down, in a large bowl. Using a sharp knife, cut downward along the cob, removing the kernels and rotating the cob a quarter turn after each cut. Reserve the cobs. Set the kernels aside. Cut one of the onions into thin slices and set aside. Cut the other onion into ½-inch dice and set aside.

CONTINUED

In a heavy soup pot, heat the vegetable oil over medium-high heat and swirl to coat the pan. Add the sliced onions and sauté, stirring frequently, until soft and just beginning to brown at the edges, 10 minutes. Add the reserved corncobs and the water. Bring to a boil, reduce the heat to a simmer, partially cover the pot, and cook until reduced to 4 cups, about 30 minutes. Using tongs, remove the cobs from the pot and discard. Pour the corn broth through a fine-mesh sieve into a clean bowl or, preferably, a 4-cup glass measure. Press down on the solids to extract as much liquid as possible. You should have 4 cups of strained broth. Set aside. Clean the soup pot.

Return the soup pot to medium heat, add the olive oil, and swirl to coat the bottom of the pot. Add the diced onion, celery, poblano chile, and thyme. Sauté the vegetables until soft but not brown, 5 to 7 minutes. Add the reserved corn kernels, cream, salt, and cayenne. Bring to a simmer and cook just until the corn is crisp-tender, 7 minutes. Add the salmon and cook at a bare simmer just until the salmon is cooked through, 3 minutes. Taste and adjust the seasoning. Divide among heated deep bowls, garnish with cilantro leaves, and serve immediately. Pass the lime wedges and squeeze a little lime juice into the soup.

COOK'S NOTE

Poblano chiles are a forest green color tinged with purple and black. They are the size of a small bell pepper but have a pointed bottom. Milder than most other chiles, poblanos still have plenty of spice, with a nice fruity quality as well. They are sometimes labeled as pasilla chiles in the market. Don't confuse them with the milder Anaheim chiles that are lighter green, longer, and more tapered in shape.

Salmon, Corn, and Potato Chowder with Fresh Thyme

Suggested wine: California or French chardonnay; dry chenin blanc

In this recipe, I skillet-toast the fresh corn for an added depth of flavor, and use fresh herbs, always my preference over dried ones. If you are into trimming calories, know you can use as little as one strip of bacon and still get that bacon taste, and milk can be substituted for the half-and-half; just don't let the chowder come to a boil.

SERVES 6 AS A LIGHT SUPPER

2 ears fresh corn
½ teaspoon kosher or sea salt
3 strips bacon, finely chopped
1 yellow onion, chopped
2 russet potatoes, peeled and cut into ½-inch cubes
2 cups bottled clam juice
1 tablespoon fresh thyme leaves
2 cups half-and-half
1 salmon fillet (about 6 ounces), skin and pin bones removed *(see page 32)*, halved lengthwise
   and cut crosswise into thin slices
⅓ cup minced fresh flat-leaf parsley
Freshly ground pepper

Husk the corn and remove all the silk. Trim the bottom end of the cob so it is even and cut close to the cob. To remove the kernels from the cobs, stand an ear of corn upright on a work surface, and with a sharp knife, cut downward along the cob. Reserve the kernels; discard cobs.

Heat a nonstick skillet over medium heat. Add the corn and sauté until the kernels are lightly browned and toasted, about 3 minutes. Stir in the salt, then remove the pan from the heat.

Cook the bacon in a heavy soup pot until crisp, about 5 minutes. Using a slotted spoon, transfer the bacon to paper towels to drain. Pour off all but 2 tablespoons of the fat from the pan. Add the onion and sauté over medium heat for 1 minute, then cover and cook until soft but not brown, about 3 minutes. Add the potatoes, clam juice, and thyme. Bring to a boil. Reduce the heat to low, cover, and simmer until the potatoes are tender, 10 to 12 minutes.

Add the corn, bacon, half-and-half, and salmon to the soup pot. Cook just below a simmer until the salmon is cooked through, about 5 minutes. (The half-and-half will curdle if the soup comes to a boil.) Add the parsley and season to taste with pepper. Serve immediately.

Bell Pepper and Vine-Ripened Tomato Gazpacho with Blackened Salmon

Suggested wine: Spanish albariño or Portuguese alvarinho

With the addition of blackened salmon, this recipe is a twist on the classic Andalusian gazpacho, making it a delightful, lip-buzzing pairing perfect for summer entertaining, either lunch or dinner. True to traditional gazpacho recipes, this soup requires the reddest vine-ripened tomatoes you can find. Wait until tomatoes are at their peak of flavor in late summer. Lots of garlic, sherry vinegar, and, preferably, a fruity Spanish extra-virgin olive oil give this soup its full-bodied flavor.

Serve this soup in large, shallow soup bowls or wide-rimmed pasta bowls. This way, the square of blackened salmon sticks out, appearing to float in the center of the bowl, giving a lovely contrast between the tomato-red soup and rich, dark spice coating. The cucumber and bell pepper garnishes add a flourish of color.

SERVES 6 AS A FIRST COURSE

One (4-inch-long) piece baguette, crust removed, cut into ½-inch dice

2 large cloves garlic

¾ teaspoon ground cumin

2 teaspoons kosher or sea salt

2 teaspoons sugar

3 tablespoons sherry vinegar

3 pounds ripe tomatoes, cored and cut into eighths

⅓ cup extra-virgin olive oil

1 salmon fillet (12 ounces), skin and pin bones removed *(see page 32)*, cut into 6 equal portions, each about 2 inches square

2 to 3 tablespoons Blackening Spice *(recipe follows)*

2 tablespoons vegetable oil

Garnish

½ cucumber, peeled, halved lengthwise, seeded, and cut into ¼-inch dice

½ green bell pepper, seeded, deribbed, and cut into ¼-inch dice

½ yellow bell pepper, seeded, deribbed, and cut into ¼-inch dice

CONTINUED

Bell Pepper and Vine-Ripened Tomato Gazpacho
with Blackened Salmon *continued*

Put the bread in a small bowl and cover with water. Soak the bread for 1 minute and then drain the water. Squeeze the bread dry and set aside.

In a food processor fitted with the metal blade, process the garlic, cumin, salt, and sugar until finely chopped. Add the bread and process until finely chopped, scraping down the sides once. Add the vinegar and pulse to combine. Add half of the tomatoes and process until finely chopped. Add the remaining tomatoes and process until puréed. (Process in 2 batches, if necessary.) With the machine running, gradually add the olive oil in a thin, steady stream until the soup is completely puréed, about 1 minute.

Set a fine-mesh sieve over a bowl large enough to hold the soup. Working in batches, force the soup through the sieve using the back of a large spoon, pressing firmly on the solids to extract as much liquid as possible. Discard the solids. Taste the soup and add more salt and vinegar, if desired. Cover and refrigerate until cold, at least 3 hours. (At this point, the soup can be covered and refrigerated for up to 2 days.)

One hour before serving, coat both sides of the salmon fillets with some of the blackening spice. Set aside at room temperature. Twenty minutes before serving, heat a large, heavy skillet, preferably cast iron, over high heat until a drop of water sprinkled in the pan sizzles and evaporates immediately. Turn your exhaust fan on high. Add the vegetable oil, swirl to coat the bottom of the pan, and carefully place the salmon pieces in the pan without crowding. (Blacken the salmon in 2 batches, if necessary.) Cook the salmon undisturbed until it blackens on the first side, 2 to 3 minutes. Adjust the heat if the salmon is blackening too quickly. Turn the salmon and cook the other side until blackened and almost opaque throughout, 2 to 3 minutes longer. Transfer the salmon to a plate and set aside at room temperature for 10 minutes to cool slightly.

To serve the gazpacho, ladle a little less than 1 cup into each of 6 large, shallow soup or pasta bowls. Carefully place a piece of salmon in the center of each bowl. Scatter some of the cucumber and green and yellow pepper over the soup. Serve immediately.

BLACKENING SPICE

This recipe makes more than you'll need for the above dish, but it is a boon to the cook's pantry. Use it on other seafood such as red snapper, swordfish, catfish, shrimp, and scallops. This mixture is also good when rubbed into burgers, flank steak, and pork tenderloin. In addition to the blackening method described above, use this rub when grilling.

2 tablespoons kosher salt
2 tablespoons sugar
1 tablespoon freshly ground pepper
1 tablespoon plus 1 teaspoon cayenne pepper
2 tablespoons paprika
1 tablespoon dried thyme
1 tablespoon dried oregano

Combine the salt, sugar, pepper, cayenne, paprika, thyme, and oregano in a small bowl. Stir well to blend. Store in an airtight jar in a cool, dark place for up to 6 months.

MAKES ABOUT ⅔ CUP

Thai Coconut Soup with Salmon, Ginger, and Lemongrass

Suggested wine: Alsatian or Oregon pinot gris; riesling; gewürztraminer

Don't be discouraged from making this soup because of the long list of ingredients—this is a quick one-pot meal. I purposely cook the rice noodles first so the pot can be rinsed and reused. (I love to cook, dislike doing dishes, and am always trying to figure out handy cleanup-saving methods!) If your supermarket doesn't have all the ingredients you need, either head to an Asian market to pick up supplies or order them online. The curry pastes will keep indefinitely in the refrigerator. Rice noodles and Thai fish sauce are a boon to have in the pantry. Kaffir lime leaves and lemongrass will keep for a couple of weeks in the refrigerator or can be frozen.

SERVES 4 AS A LIGHT SUPPER

6 ounces rice vermicelli *(see Cook's Notes)*

1 teaspoon kosher or sea salt

2 tablespoons vegetable oil

1 tablespoon peeled and minced fresh ginger

1 large clove garlic, minced

1 small yellow onion, halved lengthwise and cut into thin wedges

¼ teaspoon Thai red curry paste *(see Cook's Notes)*

2 teaspoons Thai yellow curry paste *(see Cook's Notes)*

1 can (13.5 ounces) unsweetened coconut milk

4 cups low-sodium chicken broth

1 stalk lemongrass, trimmed to about 8 inches long, halved lengthwise and flattened with the flat side of a knife

2 fresh kaffir lime leaves or 2 tablespoons fresh lime juice

2 tablespoons Thai fish sauce *(nam pla)*

1 salmon fillet (1 pound), skin and pin bones removed *(see page 32)*, cut into bite-sized pieces

Garnish

4 ounces bean sprouts, soaked in ice water for 10 minutes, then drained

¾ cup loosely packed fresh cilantro leaves

½ cup loosely packed fresh Thai basil or sweet basil leaves, shredded *(see Cook's Notes, page 76)*

Fill a 6-quart soup pot two-thirds full of water, cover, and bring to a boil over high heat. Add the rice vermicelli and salt and cook the noodles until they are soft but not completely tender, 4 minutes. (They will finish cooking once added to the soup.) Drain in a colander, rinse with cold water, drain again, and set aside. Rinse and dry the pot.

In the same pot, heat the oil over medium-low heat and swirl to coat the pan. Sauté the ginger, garlic, and onion until well coated with the oil, 1 minute. Cover the pan and cook the aromatics until softened but not brown, 2 minutes longer. Add the red and yellow curry pastes and sauté, stirring constantly, until well mixed, about 1 minute. Add the coconut milk, chicken broth, lemongrass, and lime leaves or juice. Bring to a boil. Reduce the heat to a simmer, cover, and cook for 15 minutes.

Using tongs, remove the lemongrass and lime leaves from the soup. Add the fish sauce and reserved noodles to the soup and simmer for 3 minutes. (At this point, the soup can be made up to 1 day in advance. Refrigerate, covered, then bring back to a simmer.) Add the salmon and simmer just until the fish is cooked through, about 3 minutes. Divide among warmed deep bowls and serve immediately. Pass the garnishes at the table.

COOK'S NOTES

Rice noodles are sold primarily in Asian grocery stores, but many well-stocked supermarkets also have them. Rice vermicelli, a long, thin rice noodle, is just one style. These noodles are extra-thin, about 8 inches long, and sold in cellophane packages. Within the package, the noodles are either loose or neatly bundled with a string. If you can't find rice vermicelli, the slightly wider rice stick noodles will work, too.
• Thai red and yellow curry pastes are available in small jars and cans at supermarkets or Asian grocery stores. Thai red curry paste is made of ground red chiles, herbs, and spices and packs a punch. Use more (or less) to please your taste buds.

Rice Noodle Soup with Salmon, Baby Bok Choy, and Shiitake Mushrooms

Suggested wine: German riesling

Think of this as a salmon *pho,* the Vietnamese equivalent of comforting and hearty noodle soup usually made with beef. I've skipped a few of the traditional salad garnishes to make this a quick, easy weeknight meal in a bowl, but feel free to add a few more garnishes if you like. Sliced green onions and bean sprouts would be good, and pumping up the heat with a little *sriacha,* a chile purée, will give the soup an extra kick. This soup is especially welcome on a chilly, rainy night, and I always enjoy any leftovers.

SERVES 6 AS A LIGHT SUPPER

5 ounces rice stick noodles *(see Cook's Notes, page 76)*

8 large dried shiitake mushrooms

2 tablespoons vegetable oil

1 large clove garlic, minced

1 tablespoon peeled and minced fresh ginger

1 yellow onion, halved lengthwise and cut into thin wedges

2 serrano chiles, including seeds and ribs, cut into thin rounds

8 cups low-sodium chicken broth

1 tablespoon dark soy sauce *(see Cook's Notes, page 76)*

3 star anise pods

1 large carrot, peeled and julienned

6 heads baby bok choy, halved lengthwise

1 salmon fillet (1 pound), skin and pin bones removed *(see page 32),* cut into 6 equal portions

¾ cup loosely packed fresh Thai basil or sweet basil leaves, shredded *(see Cook's Notes, page 76)*

Place the rice stick noodles in a large bowl and cover completely with hot water. Soak until softened, about 20 minutes. Rinse under warm water, drain, then cover and set aside.

CONTINUED

Rice Noodle Soup with Salmon, Baby Bok Choy,
and Shiitake Mushrooms *continued*

Place the mushrooms in a small container with a tight-fitting lid, fill the container to the top with hot water, and cover. (Using a covered container keeps the mushrooms completely submerged.) Soak the mushrooms until softened, about 20 minutes. Drain, discard the stems, and cut the mushrooms into thin strips. Set aside.

Meanwhile, in a 6-quart saucepan, heat the oil over medium-low heat and swirl to coat the pan. Sauté the garlic, ginger, onion, and chiles until soft but not brown, about 2 minutes. Add the chicken broth, soy sauce, and anise. Reduce the heat to a simmer, partially cover, and cook for 15 minutes. Add the carrot and reserved mushrooms and cook until the carrot is crisp-tender, about 5 minutes. Add the bok choy and salmon. Simmer just until the salmon is cooked through, 5 to 7 minutes longer.

Divide the noodles among 6 heated soup bowls. Ladle the soup over the noodles and top each bowl with a piece of salmon and 2 portions of bok choy. Garnish with the basil and serve immediately.

COOK'S NOTES

Rice noodles are sold primarily in Asian grocery stores, but many well-stocked supermarkets also have them. The noodles used in this recipe are Thai or Vietnamese translucent flat rice stick noodles about $^1/_4$ inch wide. The package will be labeled rice stick (ban pho or sen yai). • Dark soy sauce, sometimes labeled "black soy sauce" or "soy superior sauce," is aged for longer periods than regular soy sauce and usually contains molasses. It adds a distinct and hearty depth of flavor to a dish. My favorite brand is Koon Chun Black Soy. If you can't find dark soy sauce, substitute 1 tablespoon of regular soy mixed with $^1/_2$ teaspoon of molasses. • Thai sweet basil (bai horapha) has purplish stems, green leaves, and an aniseed aroma and flavor. It is commonly used in soups, curries, and stir-fried dishes. Though primarily sold in Asian grocery stores, many well-stocked natural foods stores carry Thai basil. Substitute Italian sweet basil if necessary.

Salmon Stock

Salmon sportfishermen who are used to gutting, cleaning, and filleting their catches—and who don't discard the salmon heads or use them for bait—can use the bones and head to make a lovely stock, beautifully pale peach in color. If you don't go salmon fishing or have friends who fish, ask your fishmonger to save you a salmon head that has the gills removed.

Salmon stock needs only an hour to simmer. Cooking the stock too long gives it a bitter taste.

MAKES 5 CUPS

1 salmon head (2 to 2½ pounds)
1 small onion, quartered
2 cloves garlic
1 carrot, cut into 2-inch chunks
1 bay leaf
3 sprigs fresh thyme
5 peppercorns
6 cups cold water
1 cup dry white wine

Rinse the salmon head and remove the gills, if necessary, leaving the gill plates intact (see page 31). Using a sharp knife, split the salmon head in half lengthwise. Place the salmon in a 6-quart saucepan and add the onion, garlic, carrot, bay leaf, thyme, and peppercorns to the pan. Add the water and wine. The fish head should be completely submerged; if not, add a bit more water. Bring the liquid to a boil and then reduce to a bare simmer. Partially cover the pot and simmer for 1 hour.

Using tongs or a large, slotted spoon, transfer the pieces of salmon and the vegetables to a large fine-mesh sieve set over a large bowl to catch all the juices. Do not press on the solids. Pour the stock through the sieve into the large bowl. Discard the solids. Let the stock cool. (To cool the stock quickly, set the bowl in a larger one filled with ice water, or a sink with about 2 inches of ice water.) Stir the stock occasionally to help cool it down. Cover and refrigerate the stock for up to 2 days. Once the stock is chilled, skim any congealed fat from the surface using the side of a large spoon. To keep the stock longer, transfer to a freezer container, allowing 1 inch of headspace, and freeze for up to 6 months.

Spaghetti with Marinated Salmon, Capers, and Herbs **80** • *Orecchiette with Smoked Salmon, Spinach, Lemon Zest, and Pine Nuts* **83** • *Farfalle with Salmon, Parsley, and Olive-Mustard Butter* **84** • *Grilled Pizza with Smoked Salmon, Red Onion, and Chive Crème Fraîche* **85** • *Grilled Pizza with Salmon, Grilled Sweet Red Peppers, and Green Onions* **88** • *Risotto with Salmon, Lemon, Fresh Herbs, and Ricotta Salata* **90** • *Risotto with Salmon, Parsley, and Green Onions* **92** • *Asian Salmon Burgers with a Green Onion and Soy Sauce Mayonnaise* **94** • *Teriyaki-Grilled Salmon Sandwiches with Hoisin and Ginger Relish* **96** • *Hot-Smoked Salmon Poorboy with Arugula and Herbed Mayonnaise* **98** • *Grilled Salmon Tacos with Chipotle Sauce* **101**

PASTA, PIZZA, RISOTTO, AND SANDWICHES

4

Spaghetti with Marinated Salmon, Capers, and Herbs

Suggested wine: Valpolicella; dolcetto

Capers, the flower buds of a bush native to the Mediterranean, are a favorite pantry staple of mine. I keep several types on the shelf or in the refrigerator. The petite capers from southern France, called nonpareils, are delicate and best used as a garnish for small bites, such as smoked salmon canapés. The larger capers, which can be as large as the tip of your little finger, are either packed in a vinegar and salt brine, or in salt. Capers packed in salt are delicious, but need to be soaked in fresh water for 30 minutes to remove the excess salt. For this pasta dish, which is so quick to assemble, I like to use larger capers preserved in brine because they only need to be rinsed and drained. Aesthetically, I like the look and "meatiness" of this size of caper with the pasta, salmon, and Parmesan.

SERVES 4 TO 6 AS A MAIN COURSE

1 salmon fillet (1¼ pounds), skin and pin bones removed (*see page 32*), cut into ¼-inch dice
¼ cup fresh lemon juice
5½ tablespoons extra-virgin olive oil
Kosher or sea salt
Freshly ground pepper
1 pound spaghetti
¼ cup capers, rinsed and drained
½ cup chopped fresh flat-leaf parsley
1¼ cups freshly grated Parmesan cheese, preferably Parmigiano-Reggiano

In a medium bowl, combine the salmon, lemon juice, 1½ tablespoons of the olive oil, ¼ teaspoon of salt, and a few grinds of pepper. Gently mix until the salmon is well coated. Set aside at room temperature to marinate for 20 minutes.

Meanwhile, fill an 8- to 10-quart stockpot two-thirds full of water and bring to a boil over high heat. Add 1 tablespoon of salt to the boiling water, then add the pasta. Stir and cook the pasta until al dente (cooked through, but still slightly chewy), about 10 minutes.

While the pasta is cooking, heat the remaining 4 tablespoons olive oil in a small sauté pan or skillet over medium heat. Add the capers and cook, stirring constantly, until crisp, about 3 minutes. Add the parsley and cook just until heated through, about 1 minute. Set aside and keep warm.

Drain the pasta in a colander, but do not rinse. Return the pasta to the stockpot and toss with the caper mixture and two-thirds of the Parmesan cheese. Add the salmon and toss gently to combine. Divide the pasta among warmed bowls, spooning any remaining salmon and capers over each serving. Sprinkle the remaining Parmesan cheese over the top and serve immediately.

Orecchiette with Smoked Salmon, Spinach, Lemon Zest, and Pine Nuts

Suggested wine: pinot grigio

A simple sauce with a minimum of ingredients, yet the end result is delicious. I love the interplay of lemon and cream; the invigorating bite of lemon cuts the richness of the cream. The dish looks lovely in a bowl, with the hints of pink salmon and the bright green spinach floating in the creamy sauce. This pasta is easy enough for a weeknight meal but special enough to serve to guests.

SERVES 4 TO 6 AS A MAIN COURSE

Kosher or sea salt
1 pound dried orecchiette pasta ("little ears")
½ cup pine nuts
1½ cups heavy (whipping) cream
12 ounces baby spinach leaves
Grated zest of 1 lemon
¼ cup fresh lemon juice
8 ounces alder-smoked or other hot-smoked salmon *(see page 124)*, skin removed,
   cut into bite-sized pieces
Freshly ground pepper

Fill an 8- to 10-quart stockpot two-thirds full of water and bring to a boil over high heat. Add 1 tablespoon of salt to the boiling water, then add the pasta. Stir and cook the pasta until al dente (cooked through, but still slightly chewy), about 10 minutes.

While the pasta is cooking, heat a dry 8-inch skillet over medium-high heat until hot but not smoking. Add the pine nuts and toast them, stirring constantly, until lightly browned, about 3 minutes. Transfer to a small plate and set aside. In a large sauté pan or skillet, bring the cream to a boil over medium heat. Add the spinach, a handful at a time, and stir just until it wilts, about 1 minute. Add the lemon zest and juice, 1 teaspoon of salt, and a few grinds of pepper. Stir to combine, then gently stir in the salmon. Cook just until heated through. Set aside and keep warm.

Drain the pasta in a colander, reserving 1 cup of the pasta cooking water. Do not rinse the pasta. Add the pasta to the pan with the sauce along with ½ cup of the reserved cooking water. Toss gently to combine and coat the pasta. Stir in the pine nuts. Add additional cooking water if the sauce seems too thick. Divide the pasta among warmed bowls, spooning any remaining salmon, spinach, and pine nuts over each serving. Serve immediately.

Farfalle with Salmon, Parsley, and Olive-Mustard Butter

Suggested wine: Soave or Orvieto

For quick weeknight meals, I love pasta dishes in which the sauce is made while the pasta cooks. This recipe requires about fifteen minutes of preparation time and ten minutes of cooking time, especially if you buy salmon that already has the skin and pin bones removed. Look for kalamata olives that are already pitted; they're sold either in bulk or in jars, and make a great pantry staple.

SERVES 4 TO 6 AS A MAIN COURSE

Kosher or sea salt
1 pound dried bow-tie (farfalle) pasta
6 tablespoons (¾ stick) unsalted butter
3 shallots, thinly sliced
⅔ cup pitted and halved kalamata olives
3 tablespoons capers, rinsed and drained
2 teaspoons Dijon mustard
1 salmon fillet (1 pound), skin and pin bones removed *(see page 32)*, cut into bite-sized pieces
⅔ cup chopped fresh flat-leaf parsley
Freshly ground pepper

Fill an 8- to 10-quart stockpot two-thirds full of water and bring to a boil over high heat. Add 1 tablespoon of salt to the boiling water, then add the pasta. Stir and cook the pasta until al dente (cooked through, but still slightly chewy), about 10 minutes.

WHILE THE PASTA IS COOKING, MAKE THE SAUCE: In a large sauté pan or skillet, melt the butter over medium heat. Add the shallots and sauté until soft but not brown, about 3 minutes. Add the olives, capers, and mustard. Stir to blend in the mustard, about 1 minute. Add the salmon and sauté just until it is cooked through, about 3 minutes. Stir in the parsley and add salt and pepper to taste. Set aside and keep warm.

Drain the pasta in a colander, but do not rinse. Add the pasta to the pan with the sauce and toss gently to combine and coat the pasta. Divide the pasta among warmed bowls, spooning any remaining salmon, olives, and capers over each serving. Serve immediately.

Grilled Pizza with Smoked Salmon, Red Onion, and Chive Crème Fraîche

Suggested wine: French chardonnay; dolcetto; Valpolicella

I've taught a lot of grill classes around the country, and students are always amazed when I grill a pizza. Though this recipe looks long and, perhaps, intimidating, it's not—and it's easy and incredibly fun to make. The two salmon pizzas I have included in my book will leave your family and guests begging for more. This recipe for pizza dough is my all-time favorite, and I've tried many; it's adapted from Alice Waters's cookbook *Chez Panisse Pasta, Pizza & Calzone*. Often, I'll double the dough recipe to make one pizza and freeze the other portion of dough just to have on hand for entertaining. I love working with dough and find it very relaxing. If, however, you're not into making pizza dough, then buy it! There are many good-quality brands on the market, sold either fresh or frozen.

SERVES 6 TO 8

1 pound Pizza Dough *(recipe follows)*, at room temperature

¼ cup snipped fresh chives

½ cup crème fraîche

½ large red onion, thinly sliced

¼ cup extra-virgin olive oil

1 teaspoon kosher or sea salt

Freshly ground pepper

4 ounces smoked salmon (lox), sliced paper-thin

2 tablespoons chopped fresh dill

Flour and cornmeal for dusting

Vegetable oil for brushing grill

Have the pizza dough covered and ready to roll out. In a small bowl, combine the chives and crème fraîche. Set aside. In a medium bowl, mix the red onion with the olive oil, salt, and a few grinds of pepper. Set aside. Remove the salmon from the refrigerator, separate the slices, and arrange on a plate ready for topping the pizza. Have the dill in a small bowl ready for garnishing.

CONTINUED

Grilled Pizza with Smoked Salmon, Red Onion, and Chive Crème Fraîche *continued*

Prepare a hot fire in a charcoal grill or preheat the center burner of a gas grill on high and the front and back or side burners to medium-low. Generously dust a pizza paddle or large rimless baking sheet with flour and then cornmeal. Have all the pizza toppings set out next to the grill before rolling out the dough.

Flatten the dough on a heavily floured work surface, sprinkling a couple of tablespoons of cornmeal over the flour. Using a rolling pin, roll the dough into a circle 12 to 13 inches in diameter. The dough should be about $1/4$ inch thick. If the dough shrinks back at the edges, gently stretch it by hand, being careful to keep the dough a uniform thickness. The dough does not need to be a perfect circle; in fact, an odd-shaped circle gives the pizza a lovely rustic look.

Using your hands and working quickly, lift and transfer the dough to the pizza paddle or baking sheet. Give the paddle a few shakes back and forth to make sure the dough isn't sticking. Brush the grill rack generously with vegetable oil. Slide the dough from the paddle onto the center of the grill rack, using a quick jerking motion with your arm. If any part of the dough folds over on itself, use a pair of tongs to unfold it. Immediately cover the grill. Grill until a crust forms and light grill marks appear, 1 to 2 minutes. Using the pizza paddle, flip the pizza crust over. Spread the onion mixture evenly over the lightly charred crust. Using a spoon, drop dollops of the crème fraîche mixture over the onions. Cover the grill and bake the pizza until nicely browned and crisp on the bottom and at the edges, about 7 minutes. Check the pizza after about 3 minutes. If the pizza is browning too quickly, slide it over to the cooler part of the grill to finish baking. Arrange the slices of lox over the onion mixture and garnish with the dill. Cover the grill and bake 1 minute longer. Remove any excess flour and cornmeal from the pizza paddle or baking sheet, and use it to transfer the pizza to a cutting board. Slice the pizza into wedges and serve immediately.

PIZZA DOUGH

I have been using this recipe for years, whether I am baking or grilling a pizza. It is the best pizza dough I know. The dough is easy to work with, the texture and crispness of the crust are fabulous, and the subtle flavor that comes from the addition of rye flour makes the crust distinct and delicious. Look for rye flour in bulk at a natural foods store. Substitute whole-wheat flour, if need be.

1 package (2 1/4 teaspoons) active dry yeast

3/4 cup lukewarm water

1/4 cup rye flour

1 tablespoon milk

2 tablespoons olive oil, plus more for oiling the bowl

3/4 teaspoon kosher or sea salt

1 3/4 cups unbleached all-purpose flour, plus more for dusting

BEGIN BY MAKING A SPONGE: In a medium bowl, dissolve the yeast in 1/4 cup of the water. Add the rye flour and stir with a wooden spoon or rubber spatula to combine. Cover with plastic wrap and allow to rise in a warm place for 20 to 30 minutes.

To make the dough, add the remaining 1/2 cup water, the milk, oil, salt, and 1 3/4 cups flour to the sponge. Using a wooden spoon, mix the dough, incorporating as much of the flour as possible. Turn the dough out on a lightly floured work surface and knead until soft and elastic, 10 to 12 minutes. It will still be a little sticky but shouldn't stick to your hands. Add only a minimum amount of flour to the work surface to keep the dough from sticking.

Lightly oil a large bowl. Add the dough and turn to coat all sides. Cover the bowl with plastic wrap and then place a clean, damp linen towel over the top. Set the bowl in a warm spot (a pilot-heated oven is a good spot, or an electric oven turned to 150°F for 5 minutes and then turned off). Allow the dough to rise until doubled in volume, about 2 hours. Punch down the dough, cover it, and allow the dough to rise for another 40 minutes. The dough is now ready to be rolled out. (If you want to make the pizza dough ahead, after the first rising, the dough can be punched down and placed in a large lock-top plastic freezer bag. Refrigerate the dough for up to 12 hours. Bring the dough to room temperature before completing the final rise. Alternatively, freeze the dough for up to 3 months. Thaw overnight in the refrigerator and then bring the dough to room temperature before completing the final rise.)

MAKES 1 POUND DOUGH, ENOUGH FOR ONE 12-INCH PIZZA

Grilled Pizza with Salmon, Grilled Sweet Red Peppers, and Green Onions

Suggested wine: rosé from the Loire Valley

Perfect for casual summer parties, everyone enjoys watching a pizza being grilled. In fact, you'll have your friends and family wanting to help! If you feel ambitious, make two different pizzas. Or, start your party with one pizza and then make salmon burgers on the grill to follow. Make a great potato salad, grill some corn, serve a big tossed salad, and all the activity will center around the grill and being outside.

SERVES 6 TO 8

1 pound Pizza Dough *(page 86),* at room temperature

Vegetable oil for brushing

6 green onions, including green tops

2 red bell peppers

1 salmon fillet (8 ounces), skin and pin bones removed *(see page 32),* cut into bite-sized pieces

3 shallots, thinly sliced

¼ cup chopped fresh flat-leaf parsley

2 tablespoons chopped fresh oregano

3 tablespoons capers, rinsed and drained

3 tablespoons fresh lemon juice

5 tablespoons extra-virgin olive oil

1 teaspoon kosher or sea salt

Freshly ground pepper

Flour and cornmeal for dusting

Have the pizza dough covered and ready to roll out.

Prepare a hot fire in a charcoal grill or preheat the center burner of a gas grill on high and the front and back or side burners to medium–low. Brush the grill rack with vegetable oil. Grill the green onions until lightly charred on all sides. Transfer to a plate and set aside. At the same time, grill the peppers, turning frequently, until the skin blisters and chars on all sides. Remove the peppers from the grill. Enclose each pepper in a damp paper towel and place the peppers in a plastic bag for 7 to 10 minutes. Use the paper towels to rub off the skin. Cut the peppers in half, discard the core, seeds, and ribs, and cut lengthwise into thin strips. Set aside.

In a medium bowl, gently mix together the salmon, shallots, parsley, oregano, capers, lemon juice, olive oil, salt, and a few grinds of pepper. Set aside to marinate.

Generously dust a pizza paddle or large rimless baking sheet with flour and then cornmeal. Have all the pizza toppings set out next to the grill before rolling out the dough.

Flatten the dough on a heavily floured work surface, sprinkling 2 tablespoons of cornmeal over the flour. Using a rolling pin, roll the dough into a circle 12 to 13 inches in diameter. The dough should be about $\frac{1}{4}$ inch thick. If the dough shrinks back at the edges, gently stretch it by hand, being careful to keep the dough a uniform thickness. The dough does not need to be a perfect circle; in fact, an odd-shaped circle gives the pizza a lovely rustic look.

Using your hands and working quickly, lift and transfer the dough to the pizza paddle or baking sheet. Give the paddle a few shakes back and forth to make sure the dough isn't sticking. Brush the grill rack generously with more vegetable oil. Slide the dough from the paddle onto the center of the grill rack using a quick jerking motion with your arm. If any part of the dough folds over on itself, use a pair of tongs to unfold it. Immediately cover the grill. Grill until a crust forms and light grill marks appear, 1 to 2 minutes. Using the pizza paddle, flip the pizza crust over. Spread the salmon mixture evenly over the lightly charred crust. Cover the grill and bake the pizza until nicely browned and crisp on the bottom and at the edges, about 7 minutes. Check the pizza after about 3 minutes. If the pizza is browning too quickly, slide it over to the cooler part of the grill to finish baking. Arrange the peppers and green onions over the salmon mixture. Cover the grill and bake 1 minute longer. Remove any excess flour and cornmeal from the pizza paddle or baking sheet, and use it to transfer the pizza to a cutting board. Slice the pizza into wedges and serve immediately.

Risotto with Salmon, Lemon, Fresh Herbs, and Ricotta Salata

Suggested wine: Orvieto; Friuli

Fresh herbs, a touch of lemon, and a sprinkling of ricotta salata cheese enhance the delicate flavor of salmon, making this dish not only outstanding and colorful, but also rich and heavenly with the addition of cream and cheese. Serve this as a main course with simple accompaniments such as steamed or roasted asparagus, or a salad of field greens with radicchio, along with a crusty baguette.

SERVES 4 AS A MAIN COURSE

5 cups Salmon Stock *(page 77)* or canned low-sodium chicken broth

3 tablespoons olive oil

½ cup diced white onion

1 clove garlic, minced

1½ cups Arborio rice *(see Cook's Note, page 93)*

½ cup dry white wine

1 salmon fillet (12 ounces), skin and pin bones removed *(see page 32)*, cut into bite-sized pieces

Grated zest of 1 lemon

1 tablespoon fresh lemon juice

3 tablespoons chopped fresh mint

3 tablespoons chopped fresh flat-leaf parsley

2 tablespoons chopped fresh tarragon

Kosher or sea salt

Freshly ground pepper

3 ounces ricotta salata cheese, crumbled *(see Cook's Note)*

In a 2-quart saucepan, bring the stock or broth to a simmer. In a heavy 4-quart saucepan, heat the oil over medium heat and sauté the onion and garlic until translucent but not brown, about 3 minutes. Add the rice and stir until the grains are well coated with oil, about 1 minute. Add the wine, let it come to a boil, and cook, stirring constantly, until most of the wine evaporates.

Add ½ cup of the stock or broth to the rice and cook, stirring frequently, until the rice has almost completely absorbed the liquid. Adjust the heat so the risotto is kept at a slow simmer. Repeat, adding ½ cup of the liquid at a time, stirring until it is almost fully absorbed before

adding more. Reserve $1/4$ cup of the liquid for adding at the end. After about 18 minutes, the rice will be plump, creamy, and cooked through but still slightly chewy. Stir in the salmon and the remaining $1/4$ cup of the stock or broth. Stir gently until the salmon is cooked through, about 3 minutes. Stir in the lemon zest, lemon juice, and fresh herbs. Season to taste with salt and pepper.

Spoon the risotto into warmed shallow bowls. Garnish each serving with some of the cheese and serve immediately.

COOK'S NOTE

Ricotta salata is a pure white, firm, rindless cheese that originated in Sicily but is made in the United States as well. Made from lightly salted sheep's milk, it is aged for a minimum of three months. It has a nutty, sweet milky flavor and is ideal for grating, slicing, or crumbling. Use it in salads, on pizzas, and especially in pasta and risotto dishes.

Risotto with Salmon, Parsley, and Green Onions

Suggested wine: pinot grigio

After a long day of work, sipping a glass of white wine while stirring risotto is relaxing. Ten minutes with a knife and cutting board and twenty minutes at the stove are all you need for this comforting dish. You could even use leftover roast or poached salmon in this risotto. Since the salmon is already cooked, just stir until it is heated through.

SERVES 4 AS A MAIN COURSE

5 cups Salmon Stock *(page 77)* or canned low-sodium chicken broth
3 tablespoons olive oil
½ cup diced white onion
1½ cups Arborio rice *(see Cook's Note)*
½ cup dry white wine
1 salmon fillet (12 ounces), skin and pin bones removed *(see page 32)*, cut into bite-sized pieces
⅓ cup minced fresh flat-leaf parsley
½ cup heavy (whipping) cream
2 tablespoons finely chopped green onion tops
Kosher or sea salt
Freshly ground pepper

In a 2-quart saucepan, bring the stock or broth to a simmer. In a heavy 4-quart saucepan, heat the oil over medium heat and sauté the onion until translucent but not brown, about 3 minutes. Add the rice and stir until the grains are well coated with oil, about 1 minute. Add the wine, let it come to a boil, and then cook, stirring constantly, until most of the wine evaporates.

Add ½ cup of the stock or broth to the rice and cook, stirring frequently, until the rice has almost completely absorbed the liquid. Adjust the heat so the risotto is kept at a slow simmer. Repeat, adding ½ cup of the liquid at a time, always stirring until it is almost fully absorbed before adding more. Reserve $1/4$ cup of the liquid for adding at the end. After about 18 minutes, the rice will be plump, creamy, and cooked through but still slightly chewy. Stir in the salmon, parsley, cream, and the remaining $1/4$ cup of the stock or broth. Stir gently until the salmon is cooked through, about 3 minutes. Stir in the green onions. Season to taste with salt and pepper.

Spoon the risotto into warmed shallow bowls and serve immediately.

COOK'S NOTE

Arborio rice is an oval-shaped short-grain white rice high in starch that is traditionally used for risotto. Look in the grain section of your supermarket for Arborio rice. Otherwise, it is readily available at specialty stores carrying Italian foodstuffs.

Asian Salmon Burgers with a Green Onion and Soy Sauce Mayonnaise

Suggested wine: German riesling; Spanish albariño or Portuguese alvarinho

What a delicious change from traditional beef burgers! Packed with ginger, garlic, green onions, and cilantro, these salmon burgers are light, juicy, and look gorgeous on a toasted bun. The recipe calls for browning the burgers in a pan, an easy stovetop method, but they can also be grilled with terrific results. Prepare a medium-hot fire in a charcoal grill or preheat a gas grill on medium-high. Oil the grill racks and rub the burgers lightly with vegetable oil before placing them on the grill. Keep the grill covered. The cooking time will be about the same as panfrying, about 3 minutes per side. The burgers will pick up a bit of a smoky flavor and have great-looking grill marks. The recipe easily doubles or triples for a crowd.

SERVES 4

1 salmon fillet (1 pound), skin and pin bones removed *(see page 32)*, cut into 1-inch pieces
1 tablespoon peeled and minced fresh ginger
1½ tablespoons minced garlic
2 green onions, including 2 inches of green tops, very thinly sliced
2 tablespoons chopped fresh cilantro
1 teaspoon kosher or sea salt
1½ tablespoons fresh lemon juice
2 tablespoons soy sauce
½ cup cracker meal
2 large eggs, lightly beaten
2 tablespoons vegetable oil
4 sesame-seed hamburger buns, split and toasted
4 lettuce leaves
Green Onion and Soy Sauce Mayonnaise *(recipe follows)*

In a food processor fitted with the metal blade, pulse the salmon until coarsely ground, scraping down the sides of the work bowl once or twice. (Be careful; it's easy to go from chopped to a mashed paste in seconds!) Transfer the salmon to a medium bowl. Add the ginger, garlic, green onions, cilantro, salt, lemon juice, and soy sauce. Using a rubber spatula, mix to combine. Mix in the cracker meal and then add the eggs. Stir to combine.

Dividing the salmon mixture evenly, form into four 1-inch-thick patties. Refrigerate for at least 20 minutes before cooking. (The patties can be prepared up to 8 hours ahead. Transfer to a covered container and refrigerate.)

In a large, heavy skillet, preferably cast iron, heat the oil over medium-high heat and swirl to coat the pan. (You can also use a grill pan.) Add the salmon patties and cook until golden brown on one side, about 3 minutes. Turn and cook until opaque throughout and golden brown on the other side, about 3 minutes longer. Serve the salmon burgers on the toasted buns with the lettuce and mayonnaise.

GREEN ONION AND SOY SAUCE MAYONNAISE

½ cup mayonnaise
1 green onion, including green tops, very thinly sliced
1 teaspoon fresh lemon juice
2 teaspoons soy sauce

In a small bowl, mix together the mayonnaise, green onion, lemon juice, and soy sauce until well blended. Cover and refrigerate for up to 1 day.

MAKES ABOUT ⅔ CUP

Teriyaki-Grilled Salmon Sandwiches with Hoisin and Ginger Relish

Suggested wine: riesling; Spanish albariño or Portuguese alvarinho

Here's an Asian twist on a gutsy salmon sandwich. Boldly infused with big hits of ginger and garlic, this teriyaki-marinated salmon is grilled to perfection, giving a smoky-sweet quality to the fish. As a counterpoint and a delicious addition to the sandwich, a cool and crunchy hoisin-and-ginger relish is slathered on a crusty baguette. The sandwich is finished with a slawlike mound of shredded napa cabbage. Serve with a side of taro root chips and a little mound of pickled ginger. Add this to your repertoire for casual summer eating.

MAKES 4 SANDWICHES

Marinade

⅓ cup soy sauce

⅓ cup mirin *(see Cook's Notes, page 51)*

3 tablespoons honey

1 tablespoon Asian sesame oil

1 tablespoon peeled and minced fresh ginger

1 clove garlic, thinly sliced

4 salmon fillets (about 5 ounces each), skin on and scaled, pin bones removed *(see page 32)*

Vegetable oil for brushing

1 baguette (about 20 inches long)

Hoisin and Ginger Relish *(recipe follows)*

1 small head napa cabbage, halved lengthwise, cored, and cut crosswise into thin slices

TO MAKE THE MARINADE: In a small bowl, combine the soy sauce, mirin, honey, sesame oil, ginger, and garlic. Place the salmon in a baking dish, pour the marinade over the top, turn the salmon to coat all sides, and marinate at room temperature for 45 minutes.

Prepare a medium fire in a charcoal grill or preheat a gas grill to medium.

To grill the salmon, brush the grill grate with vegetable oil. Place the salmon, skin side up, directly over the medium fire. Cover the grill and cook on one side until beautiful grill marks are etched across the fillets, about 4 minutes. Baste the salmon with some of the marinade and then turn and cover again. Cook until the salmon is almost opaque throughout, but still very moist, or an instant-read thermometer inserted in the center registers between 125° and 130°F, about 5 minutes more. Transfer to a plate and set aside.

To assemble the sandwiches, cut the baguette crosswise into 4 sections, each approximately 5 inches in length. Split each section in half lengthwise, cutting almost all the way but not completely through the crust on the opposite side. Use your fingers to pull out and discard some of the soft bread, hollowing out a canoe-shaped section on each side. Spoon some of the hoisin relish on both sides of each sandwich, generously filling the hollowed-out sections. Place a piece of salmon on top of the bottom piece of bread. Stuff some napa cabbage along the length of each sandwich. Serve immediately.

HOISIN AND GINGER RELISH

⅓ cup mayonnaise
⅓ cup hoisin sauce
1 tablespoon peeled and minced fresh ginger
2 jalapeno chiles, seeded, deribbed, and minced
1 cup finely diced daikon
1 cup finely diced jicama
2 green onions, including green tops, diced
Juice of 1 lime

In a medium bowl, combine the mayonnaise, hoisin, ginger, and chiles. Stir in the daikon, jicama, and green onions. Cover and refrigerate for up to 1 day. Stir in the lime juice just before assembling the sandwiches.

MAKES ABOUT 2½ CUPS

Hot-Smoked Salmon Poorboy with Arugula and Herbed Mayonnaise

Suggested wine: Austrian grüner veltliner; domestic sparkling wine

These sandwiches are simply fabulous! This dynamite combination of hot-smoked salmon, shallot- and herb-infused mayonnaise, and spicy arugula makes this one of the best poorboy sandwiches I know. Make these ahead, individually wrap them, and take them along for summer picnics at the beach or outdoor concerts. Add a fruit salad and/or bean or pasta salad to the picnic basket and you're set. If you can't find demi-baguettes, buy a large baguette and cut it into fourths crosswise or use a loaf of ciabatta.

MAKES 4 SANDWICHES

1 heaping tablespoon alder wood chips

Nonstick cooking spray

1 center-cut salmon fillet (12 ounces), skin on and scaled, pin bones removed, skin dried by wiping with a knife *(see page 32)*

1 tablespoon extra-virgin olive oil

¼ teaspoon minced garlic

Freshly ground pepper

Four (10-inch-long) demi-baguettes

Herbed Mayonnaise *(recipe follows)*

1 bunch arugula (about 4 ounces), stemmed

Using a stovetop smoker or wok, place the wood chips in a small pile in the center of the pan. Place a drip tray, covered with aluminum foil, on top of the chips. If using a wok, set a large sheet of aluminum foil loosely in place over the wood chips. Place a wire rack, sprayed with nonstick spray, on top of the drip tray or foil. Arrange the salmon on top. Mix together the olive oil and garlic. Rub over the salmon, then sprinkle with a little pepper. Slide the lid on the stovetop smoker or cover the wok, leaving it slightly open, and then place the smoker over medium heat. When the first wisp of smoke appears, close the lid. Smoke the salmon for 17 minutes. Turn the heat off and leave the salmon in the smoker, covered, for an additional 5 minutes.

CONTINUED

Hot-Smoked Salmon Poorboy with Arugula
and Herbed Mayonnaise *continued*

To assemble the sandwiches, split the baguettes in half lengthwise, cutting almost all the way but not completely through the crust on the opposite side. Spread about 3 tablespoonfuls of the herbed mayonnaise down the length of each baguette. Cut the salmon into 4 long pieces and arrange on top of the mayonnaise. Stuff some arugula along the length of each sandwich. Serve immediately, or wrap individually and refrigerate. Remove from the refrigerator 20 minutes before serving.

HERBED MAYONNAISE

½ cup mayonnaise

¼ cup sour cream

1 teaspoon grated lemon zest

1 teaspoon fresh lemon juice

1 teaspoon Dijon mustard

¼ teaspoon kosher or sea salt

Freshly ground pepper

1½ tablespoons minced shallot

3 tablespoons minced fresh basil (about 15 leaves)

2 tablespoons minced fresh flat-leaf parsley

1 teaspoon minced fresh thyme

In a small bowl, combine the mayonnaise, sour cream, lemon zest and juice, mustard, salt, and a few grinds of pepper. Stir to combine. Add the shallot, basil, parsley, and thyme. Taste and adjust the seasoning. Cover and refrigerate for up to 2 days.

MAKES ABOUT 1 CUP

Grilled Salmon Tacos with Chipotle Sauce

Suggested wine: Spanish albariño or Portuguese alvarinho; Oregon pinot gris

This is one of my family's favorites. I always have a jar of the Blackening Spice (page 71) rub used in this recipe on the pantry shelf, which makes this meal quick and simple. I can get every-thing made and assembled while the grill is preheating and the salmon is cooking. Then we all sit down with the bowls and plates of salmon, tortillas, sauce, and vegetables in the center of the table and help ourselves. It's great fun, convivial, and casual. Think about making these tacos when you have leftover grilled salmon, too.

MAKES 12 TORTILLAS; SERVES 6

1 salmon fillet (1½ pounds), skin on and scaled, pin bones removed *(see page 32)*

2 tablespoons olive oil

¼ cup Blackening Spice *(page 71)*

Vegetable oil for brushing

12 corn tortillas

½ head cabbage (8 ounces), cored and finely shredded (about 5 cups)

3 green onions, including green tops, quartered lengthwise and cut into 1-inch lengths

3 tablespoons fresh lime juice

2 ripe tomatoes, halved crosswise, cored, seeded, and cut into ¼-inch dice

Chipotle Sauce *(recipe follows)*

Preheat the oven to 250°F.

Prepare a medium fire in a charcoal grill or preheat a gas grill to medium. Arrange the salmon, skin side up, on a rimmed baking sheet. Oil the skin generously with about 1 tablespoon of the olive oil. Turn the salmon over and rub the flesh side all over with the blackening spice. Using your fingertips, lightly dab the remaining olive oil over the blackening spice.

When ready to grill, brush the grill grate generously with vegetable oil. Grill the salmon, skin side up, directly over the fire. Cover the grill and cook on one side for 4 minutes. Turn and

CONTINUED

cover again. Cook until almost opaque throughout, but still very moist, or an instant-read thermometer inserted in the center registers 125° to 130°F, about 5 minutes more. Transfer to a cutting board and cool slightly.

Meanwhile, place the tortillas in a covered heatproof container or sealed aluminum foil packet. Warm the tortillas in the oven for 15 minutes before serving.

In a medium serving bowl, toss together the cabbage, green onions, and lime juice. Place the tomatoes in a small serving bowl. Slice the salmon crosswise into 12 strips, lift the salmon off its skin, and arrange on a warm serving plate. Discard the skin. Transfer the warm tortillas to a serving plate. Let each diner assemble his or her own tortilla. To assemble, spread a generous spoonful of sauce down the middle of a tortilla, arrange a strip of salmon on top, mound with a bit of the cabbage mixture, and garnish with some diced tomatoes.

CHIPOTLE SAUCE

1 cup mayonnaise

3 tablespoons buttermilk or sour cream

2 minced canned chipotle chiles in adobo sauce

2 tablespoons minced fresh cilantro

1/4 teaspoon kosher or sea salt

In a small serving bowl, mix together the mayonnaise, buttermilk or sour cream, chipotle chiles, cilantro, and salt. Cover and set aside for up to 45 minutes, or cover and refrigerate for up to 3 days.

MAKES 1 1/4 CUPS

Pan-Roasted Salmon with Warm French Lentil Salad **106** · *Spinach Salad with Blackened Salmon, Oranges,*

and Red Onion **108** · *Shaved Fennel, Lemon, and Arugula Salad, with Pan-Seared Salmon* **110** ·

Lemon-Grilled Salmon Caesar Salad **112** · *Composed Salad of Asparagus and Salmon with a Lemon Vinaigrette*

and Toasted Pine Nuts **115** · *Asian Noodle Salad with Sesame-Crusted Salmon* **117** · *Salmon and*

Grill-Roasted Sweet Corn Salad **121** · *Wild Rice Salad with Hot-Smoked Salmon, Mango, Green Onions,*

and Toasted Hazelnuts **123** · *Chopped Salad with Salmon, Hard-Cooked Eggs, Potatoes, Frisée, Radish,*

and Avocado **125** · *Hot-Smoked Salmon Salad with Curly Endive and Bacon* **127**

MAIN-COURSE SALADS

Pan-Roasted Salmon with Warm French Lentil Salad

Suggested wine: Oregon pinot noir or Beaujolais

Salmon with lentils is a divine combination. Lovely slate-green, robust-flavored *lentilles de Puy* are tossed with a lemony, tarragon-infused vinaigrette and blended with crisply cooked vegetables. A simply seasoned fillet of salmon is pan-roasted and nestled on top of the warm lentil mixture. This is a perfect main-course salad for casual entertaining or for a weeknight dinner with a crusty baguette and a glass of pinot noir. You'll have dinner on the table in less than 40 minutes.

SERVES 4

Vinaigrette

¼ cup extra-virgin olive oil

1 teaspoon grated lemon zest

2 tablespoons fresh lemon juice

2 cloves garlic, minced

2 tablespoons chopped fresh tarragon

½ teaspoon sugar

1 teaspoon kosher or sea salt

Freshly ground pepper

1 cup French green lentils *(lentilles de Puy); see Cook's Note*

4 salmon fillets (about 5 ounces each), skin on and scaled, pin bones removed,
   skin dried by wiping with a knife *(see pages 30–33)*

Kosher or sea salt

Freshly ground pepper

5 tablespoons olive oil

2 large carrots, peeled and cut into ¼-inch dice

2 shallots, cut into ¼-inch dice

1 celery stalk, cut into ¼-inch dice

1 red bell pepper, seeded, deribbed, and cut into ¼-inch dice

Arrange an oven rack in the center of the oven and preheat the oven to 450°F.

TO MAKE THE VINAIGRETTE: In a small jar with a tight-fitting lid, combine the extra-virgin olive oil, lemon zest and juice, garlic, tarragon, sugar, salt, and lots of pepper. (Several good grinds of pepper make the vinaigrette taste robust, a perfect complement to the lentils.) Cover tightly and shake vigorously to blend. Taste and adjust the seasoning. Set aside.

Fill a 3-quart saucepan two-thirds full of cold water, add the lentils, and bring to a simmer over medium heat. Cook, uncovered, just until tender, 15 to 18 minutes. Meanwhile, season the salmon with a little salt and pepper. Have ready 2 large skillets: a large, ovenproof skillet, preferably cast iron, for cooking the salmon; and a large skillet for sautéing the vegetables.

When the lentils are tender, drain them thoroughly but do not rinse. Transfer to a large bowl and set aside. In the ovenproof skillet, heat 2 tablespoons of the olive oil over high heat until almost smoking. Swirl to coat the pan and then add the salmon, skin side down. Cook over high heat until the skin is browned and crisp, about 4 minutes. After about 3 minutes, shake the pan once to make sure the fillets aren't sticking. Carefully turn the fillets, then transfer the skillet to the oven and roast the salmon until almost opaque throughout, about 4 minutes. Set aside.

As soon as the salmon goes into the oven, place the other skillet over high heat and add the remaining 3 tablespoons olive oil. Swirl to coat the pan and add the carrots, shallots, celery, and bell pepper. Sauté, stirring frequently, until the vegetables are crisp-tender and just beginning to brown at the edges, about 7 minutes. Season lightly with salt and pepper. Add the vegetables to the bowl with the lentils and stir gently to mix.

Give the dressing a last-minute shake and pour it over the lentil mixture. Toss gently. Divide the lentil mixture among 4 dinner plates. Place a salmon fillet in the center, on top of the lentils, and serve immediately.

COOK'S NOTE

Lentilles de Puy *from France's Haute-Loire region are prized for their earthy, robust flavor. If cooked just until tender, they remain firm and retain their lovely petite shape without bursting. They have a dark slate-green exterior and creamy yellow interior. American lentil farmers have started growing heirloom varieties, including ones similar to* lentilles de Puy. *Look for these at gourmet or natural foods stores.*

Spinach Salad with Blackened Salmon, Oranges, and Red Onion

Suggested wine or beverage: Austrian grüner veltliner; Bloody Mary

A spinach salad, colorfully mixed with red bell pepper, thinly sliced red onion, and segments of navel orange, makes a terrific salad all on its own, but when a fabulous serving of blackened salmon is placed on top, you've got a main–course salad worth raving about. This salad is easy enough to serve for a weeknight meal, or at a Sunday brunch. It's dynamite with a Bloody Mary!

Save yourself some time and buy the packaged, prewashed, and trimmed baby spinach. The greens stay fresh for several days in the refrigerator.

SERVES 4

4 salmon fillets (about 5 ounces each), skin and pin bones removed *(see page 32)*
2 tablespoons Blackening Spice *(page 71)*
7 cups (about 6 ounces) lightly packed baby spinach leaves
1 cup thinly sliced red onion
1 red bell pepper, halved lengthwise, seeded, deribbed, and cut into long, thin slices
2 navel oranges, peeled and white pith removed, cut into segments
¼ cup extra-virgin olive oil
1 tablespoon balsamic vinegar
1 teaspoon whole-grain mustard
½ teaspoon sugar
½ teaspoon kosher or sea salt
Freshly ground pepper
2 tablespoons vegetable oil

One hour before serving, coat both sides of the salmon fillets with the blackening spice. Set aside at room temperature. Meanwhile, place the spinach, onion, and bell pepper in a large salad bowl. Put the oranges in a small bowl.

In a small jar with a tight–fitting lid, combine the olive oil, vinegar, mustard, sugar, salt, and pepper to taste. Cover tightly and shake vigorously to blend. Taste and adjust the seasoning.

Twenty minutes before serving, heat a large, heavy skillet, preferably cast iron, over high heat until a drop of water sprinkled in the pan sizzles and evaporates immediately. Turn your exhaust fan on high. Add the vegetable oil, swirl to coat the bottom of the pan, and then carefully place the salmon fillets in the pan without crowding. Cook the salmon undisturbed until it blackens on the first side, 2 to 3 minutes. Adjust the heat if the salmon is blackening too quickly. Turn the salmon and cook the other side until blackened and almost opaque throughout, but still very moist, about 3 minutes longer. Transfer the salmon to a plate and set aside at room temperature for 10 minutes to cool slightly.

When ready to serve, add the orange segments to the salad bowl, give the dressing a last-minute shake, and pour over the salad. Toss gently. Arrange the salad on 4 dinner plates. Place a salmon fillet in the center, on top of the salad, and serve immediately.

Shaved Fennel, Lemon, and Arugula Salad, with Pan-Seared Salmon

Suggested wine: Champagne; domestic sparkling wine; Rhône white

I've paired salmon and fennel several times in this book and there is a reason for it: they make a gorgeous marriage of taste, texture, and color. Here the fennel is thinly sliced, partnered with peppery arugula, and tossed with a lemon vinaigrette. A quickly pan-seared salmon fillet sits on top of a mound of this slawlike salad. A quick garnish with fennel fronds and you have a main-course salad worthy of company, yet simple and easy enough for a family meal.

SERVES 4

Vinaigrette

¼ cup extra-virgin olive oil

1 teaspoon grated lemon zest

2 tablespoons fresh lemon juice

1 clove garlic, minced

½ teaspoon sugar

¾ teaspoon kosher or sea salt

Freshly ground pepper

3 cups thinly sliced fennel bulb (fronds reserved)

2 bunches arugula (about 8 ounces total), stemmed

4 salmon fillets (about 5 ounces each), skin on and scaled, pin bones removed,
   skin dried by wiping with a knife *(see pages 30–33)*

Kosher or sea salt

Freshly ground pepper

3 tablespoons olive oil for sautéing

TO MAKE THE VINAIGRETTE: In a small jar with a tight-fitting lid, combine the extra-virgin olive oil, lemon zest and juice, garlic, sugar, salt, and lots of pepper. (Several good grinds of pepper make the vinaigrette taste robust, a perfect complement to the fennel.) Cover tightly and shake vigorously to blend. Taste and adjust the seasoning. Set aside.

Chop the fennel fronds and measure out ⅓ cup. In a large bowl, combine the fennel, ¼ cup of the fennel fronds (saving the rest for garnish), and the arugula. Toss lightly to mix and set aside.

Season the salmon on all sides with a little salt and pepper. Place a large, heavy skillet over medium-high heat. When the skillet is hot, add the 3 tablespoons of olive oil and swirl to coat the pan. Add the salmon, skin side down, and cook until the skin is crisp, about 4 minutes. Carefully turn the salmon and cook until the fillets are almost opaque throughout, but still very moist, or an instant-read thermometer inserted in the center registers 125° to 130°F, about 4 minutes more. Transfer to a warm plate and set aside while you toss the salad.

Shake the dressing vigorously again and then toss the salad with it. Arrange the salad on 4 dinner plates. Place a salmon fillet in the center, on top of the salad, garnish with the remaining fennel fronds, and serve immediately.

Lemon–Grilled Salmon Caesar Salad

Suggested wine: Champagne; domestic sparkling wine; dry chenin blanc

A classic with a twist. This Caesar is powered with garlic, touched with anchovy, and elegantly adorned with a glistening lemon–infused fillet of grilled salmon. A generous dose of croutons gives crunch to every bite. I prefer to use hearts of romaine because the inner leaves are so much crunchier. If the packaged hearts of romaine are small, use 3 or 4 total. I like big Caesar salads so am always generous with the amount of greens.

SERVES 4

Marinade

2½ tablespoons olive oil

¾ tablespoon fresh lemon juice

1 clove garlic, minced

1 oil-packed anchovy fillet, patted dry and minced

¼ teaspoon kosher or sea salt

Freshly ground pepper

4 salmon fillets (about 5 ounces each), skin on and scaled, pin bones removed, skin dried by wiping with a knife *(see pages 30–33)*

Dressing

1 tablespoon minced garlic

2 oil-packed anchovy fillets, patted dry and minced

¾ teaspoon kosher or sea salt

2 tablespoons fresh lemon juice

1 very fresh large egg *(see Cook's Note)*

½ cup extra-virgin olive oil

⅓ cup freshly grated Parmigiano-Reggiano cheese

Vegetable oil for brushing

2 cups homemade or store-bought large croutons

2 to 3 large hearts of romaine lettuce, torn into bite-sized pieces

Freshly grated Parmigiano-Reggiano cheese for garnish

Freshly ground pepper

Prepare a medium-hot fire in a charcoal grill or preheat a gas grill to medium-high.

TO MAKE THE MARINADE: In a small bowl, whisk together the olive oil, lemon juice, garlic, anchovy, salt, and pepper to taste. Place the salmon in a baking dish. Add the marinade and turn the salmon to coat all sides. Set aside until the grill gets hot.

MEANWHILE, MAKE THE SALAD DRESSING: In a small bowl, whisk together the garlic, anchovies, salt, and lemon juice. Add the egg and whisk the dressing until thick, about 1 minute. Slowly drizzle in the extra-virgin olive oil, whisking vigorously to thicken. Whisk in the cheese. Taste and adjust the seasoning. Set aside. (The dressing can also be made in a blender or food processor.)

To grill the salmon, brush the grill grate with vegetable oil. Place the salmon, skin side up, directly over the medium-hot fire. Cover the grill and cook on one side until beautiful grill marks are etched across the fillets, about 4 minutes. Turn and cover again. Cook until the salmon is almost opaque throughout, but still very moist, or an instant-read thermometer inserted in the center registers between 125° and 130°F, about 5 minutes more. Remove the salmon from the grill and set aside.

To assemble the salad, pour half of the dressing in the bottom of an oversized bowl. Add the croutons and toss in the dressing until thoroughly coated. Add the lettuce and the remaining dressing. Toss just until coated. Divide among 4 entrée plates. Place a salmon fillet in the center, on top of the salad, and garnish with additional cheese and pepper to taste. Serve immediately.

COOK'S NOTE

If you prefer not to use a raw egg in the dressing, substitute 1 additional tablespoon of extra-virgin olive oil in place of the egg. Raw eggs in any form should not be served to children, the elderly, pregnant women, or anyone with a compromised immune system.

Composed Salad of Asparagus and Salmon with a Lemon Vinaigrette and Toasted Pine Nuts

Suggested wine: Champagne; domestic sparkling wine; Austrian grüner veltliner; sauvignon blanc

In the summer, I like to do as much cooking on the grill as possible. This main-course salad is a perfect example of how to combine efforts so just about everything is cooked outside. While the grill is preheating, I make the salad dressing and toast the pine nuts. With those ready and set aside, I can focus my attention outside, double-timing the grilling of the salmon and asparagus. As soon as the fish and veggies are done, all that is left to do is arrange the plates and serve. This is a light, simple entrée, absolutely delightful for dining al fresco on a warm summer night.

SERVES 4

Dressing
¼ cup extra-virgin olive oil
1 teaspoon grated lemon zest
2 tablespoons fresh lemon juice
1 clove garlic, minced
½ teaspoon Dijon mustard
½ teaspoon sugar
¾ teaspoon kosher or sea salt
Freshly ground pepper

½ cup pine nuts
4 salmon fillets (about 5 ounces each), skin on and scaled, pin bones removed,
  skin dried by wiping with a knife *(see pages 30–33)*
Kosher sea salt
Freshly ground pepper
2 to 3 tablespoons olive oil
28 thick spears asparagus, tough ends removed
Vegetable oil for brushing
¼ cup 1-inch-long fresh chives

CONTINUED

Composed Salad of Asparagus and Salmon with a Lemon Vinaigrette and Toasted Pine Nuts *continued*

Prepare a medium-hot fire in a charcoal grill or preheat a gas grill to medium-high.

MEANWHILE, MAKE THE SALAD DRESSING: In a small jar with a tight-fitting lid, combine the extra-virgin olive oil, lemon zest and juice, garlic, mustard, sugar, salt, and lots of pepper. (Several good grinds of pepper make the vinaigrette taste robust.) Cover tightly and shake vigorously to blend. Taste and adjust the seasoning. Set aside.

Heat a dry 8-inch skillet over medium-high heat. When hot but not smoking, add the pine nuts and toast them, stirring constantly, until lightly browned, about 3 minutes. Transfer to a small plate and set aside.

Sprinkle the salmon fillets with salt and pepper and brush all sides with some of the olive oil. Brush the asparagus spears with olive oil.

To grill the salmon and asparagus, brush the grill grate with vegetable oil. Place the salmon, skin side up, directly over the medium-hot fire. (Space the salmon so there is room to add the asparagus.) Cover the grill and cook the salmon on one side until beautiful grill marks are etched across the fillets, about 4 minutes. Turn the salmon skin side down. Arrange the asparagus in a single layer on the grill grate and cover the grill. Cook the asparagus for 3 minutes on one side, then turn the spears to cook the other side until nicely burnished and crisp-tender when pierced with a knife, about 2 minutes more. Continue cooking the salmon until it is almost opaque throughout, but still very moist, or an instant-read thermometer inserted in the center registers between 125° and 130°F, about 5 minutes more. Remove the salmon and asparagus from the grill.

To arrange the salad, fan 7 spears of asparagus on each of 4 entrée plates. Place a salmon fillet in the center and on top of the asparagus. Divide and scatter the pine nuts over each plate. Give the dressing a last-minute shake and drizzle over the salmon and asparagus, dividing evenly. Garnish with the chives and serve immediately.

Asian Noodle Salad with Sesame-Crusted Salmon

Suggested wine: riesling; sauvignon blanc

Sesame-crusted salmon, slow-roasted to perfection, pairs beautifully with this Asian noodle salad. Coating the salmon with a mixture of black and white sesame seeds adds a dramatic flair to the presentation. Look for black sesame seeds in the bulk-foods section of natural foods stores or Asian markets. Store sesame seeds in the freezer to keep them from going rancid.

SERVES 4

3 packages (2 ounces each) rice vermicelli (bean threads) *(see Cook's Note, page 53)*

4 salmon fillets (about 5 ounces each), skin and pin bones removed *(see page 32)*

1 tablespoon olive oil

Kosher or sea salt

4 teaspoons white sesame seeds

4 teaspoons black sesame seeds

¼ cup soy sauce

1 tablespoon rice vinegar

3 tablespoons Asian sesame oil

2 teaspoons sugar

2 teaspoons peeled and minced fresh ginger

1 large carrot, peeled and julienned

1 large stalk celery, julienned

2 green onions, including green tops, cut into matchsticks

½ cup packed fresh cilantro leaves

Preheat the oven to 250°F. Line a rimmed baking sheet with parchment paper.

Soak the rice vermicelli in a large bowl of warm water until softened, about 20 minutes. Drain well in a colander, shaking the colander a few times to make sure all the water is removed.

CONTINUED

Asian Noodle Salad with Sesame-Crusted Salmon *continued*

Rub each salmon fillet with olive oil and sprinkle lightly with salt. On a small plate, combine the white and black sesame seeds. Dip the top side of each salmon fillet in the sesame seeds and place on the prepared baking sheet, seed side up. Bake the salmon until the fat between the layers begins to turn whitish and opaque and the fish flakes slightly, or an instant-read thermometer inserted in the center registers between 125° and 130°F, about 20 minutes.

WHILE THE SALMON IS BAKING, MAKE THE SALAD: In a large bowl, combine the soy sauce, vinegar, sesame oil, sugar, and ginger. Add the rice vermicelli and toss until the noodles are well coated with the dressing. Add the carrot, celery, green onions, and cilantro. Toss to combine.

When the salmon is done, divide the noodle mixture among 4 entrée plates. Place a salmon fillet in the center, on top of the noodles, and serve immediately.

Salmon and Grill-Roasted Sweet Corn Salad

Suggested wine: French chardonnay

Nothing could be finer than a main-course summer salad. A perfectly seared fillet of salmon sits atop a mound of lightly dressed salad greens, showered with smoky grilled corn kernels, shavings of fennel and red onion, dots of tiny grape tomatoes, and flecks of chopped fresh herbs.

SERVES 4

3 ears fresh corn

3 tablespoons olive oil

4 salmon fillets (about 5 ounces each), skin on and scaled, pin bones removed,
  skin dried by wiping with a knife *(see pages 30–33)*

Kosher or sea salt

Freshly ground pepper

Vegetable oil for brushing

6 cups (about 4½ ounces) lightly packed mixed baby greens

1 fennel bulb, trimmed, halved lengthwise, cored, and cut into paper-thin wedges

⅓ red onion, cut into paper-thin wedges

1 cup grape or cherry tomatoes

¼ cup minced fresh flat-leaf parsley

2 tablespoons minced fresh chives

Dressing

2 tablespoons rice vinegar

6 tablespoons extra-virgin olive oil

1 teaspoon Dijon mustard

1 teaspoon sugar

½ teaspoon kosher or sea salt

Freshly ground pepper

CONTINUED

Salmon and Grill-Roasted Sweet Corn Salad *continued*

Prepare a medium-hot fire in a charcoal grill or preheat a gas grill to medium-high.

Pull back the husk from each ear of corn without removing it from the base. Remove the silk, then brush each ear of corn lightly with half of the olive oil. Re-cover the corn with the husk, then twist the husks at the top to close.

Sprinkle the salmon fillets with salt and pepper and brush all sides with the rest of the olive oil. When the grill is hot, brush the grill grate with vegetable oil.

Place the salmon, skin side up, directly over the medium-hot fire. Arrange the corn on the grill grate directly over the fire. Cover the grill and cook the salmon and corn for about 5 minutes. Turn both the corn and salmon and cover the grill again. Cook the salmon until almost opaque throughout, but still very moist, or an instant-read thermometer inserted in the center registers 125° to 130°F, about 4 minutes more. Remove the salmon from the grill and set aside. Give the corn one more turn and continue grilling just until it begins to color, about 2 minutes longer. Remove the corn from the grill.

When the corn is cool enough to handle, remove the husks. Working with 1 ear at a time, stand it upright, stem end down, on a cutting board. Using a sharp knife, cut downward along the cob, removing the kernels and rotating the cob a quarter turn after each cut. Discard the cobs and scoop the kernels into a large bowl.

Place the baby greens, fennel, onion, tomatoes, parsley, and chives in the bowl with the corn. Toss gently to mix.

TO MAKE THE DRESSING: In a small bowl, combine the vinegar, extra-virgin olive oil, mustard, sugar, salt, and pepper to taste. Stir until well combined. Add the dressing to the salad, and toss lightly. Arrange the salad on 4 dinner plates. Place a salmon fillet in the center, on top of the salad, and serve immediately.

Wild Rice Salad with Hot-Smoked Salmon, Mango, Green Onions, and Toasted Hazelnuts

Suggested wine: Spanish albariño or Portuguese alvarinho; sauvignon blanc

Wild rice, so often served with roast turkey or chicken, is a terrific partner with salmon. I'm especially fond of pairing wild rice with hot-smoked salmon because the earthy, rustic flavor of the rice is perfect with the deep, smoky quality of the alder-smoked fish. Color plays a big role in making this salad a visual delight. The glistening pink salmon sits atop sleek brown-black grains of rice speckled with orange chunks of mango, slivers of green onions, and toasted hazelnuts. A lemon-ginger dressing pops the flavor, making this salad a standout.

SERVES 4

1½ cups wild rice

Kosher or sea salt

1 heaping tablespoon alder wood chips

Nonstick cooking spray

1 center-cut salmon fillet (about 1½ pounds), skin on and scaled, pin bones removed, skin dried by wiping with a knife *(see pages 30–33)*

Juice of ½ lemon

¼ teaspoon cayenne pepper

½ cup halved hazelnuts

1 mango, peeled, seeded, and cut into ¼-inch dice

4 green onions, including green tops, thinly sliced

Dressing

¼ cup extra-virgin olive oil

½ teaspoon grated lemon zest

2 tablespoons fresh lemon juice

1½ tablespoons soy sauce

1 teaspoon peeled and grated fresh ginger

1 small clove garlic, minced

½ teaspoon sugar

CONTINUED

Wild Rice Salad with Hot-Smoked Salmon, Mango, Green Onions, and Toasted Hazelnuts *continued*

Place the rice in a medium saucepan and add cold water to cover by 2 inches. Add $1/2$ teaspoon of salt. Bring to a boil over high heat, reduce the heat to a simmer, partially cover, and cook, stirring occasionally, until the rice is tender, 40 to 50 minutes. Drain in a sieve and rinse with cool water so the rice is cooled but not cold. Drain again. Place in a large mixing bowl.

MEANWHILE, HOT-SMOKE THE SALMON: Using a stovetop smoker or wok, place the wood chips in a small pile in the center of the pan. Place a drip tray, covered with aluminum foil, on top of the chips. (If using a wok, set a large sheet of aluminum foil loosely in place over the wood chips.) Place a wire rack, sprayed with nonstick spray, on top of the drip tray or foil. Arrange the salmon on top, squeeze the juice of $1/2$ lemon over the salmon, and then sprinkle with a little salt and the cayenne pepper. Slide the lid on the stovetop smoker or cover the wok, leaving it slightly open, and then place the smoker over medium heat. When the first wisp of smoke appears, close the lid. Smoke the salmon for 17 minutes. Turn the heat off and leave the salmon in the smoker, covered, for an additional 5 minutes. Remove the lid and set the salmon aside.

Spread the hazelnuts on a rimmed baking sheet and toast them in a preheated 350°F oven until lightly browned, about 10 minutes. Rub the nuts together in a terry kitchen towel to remove the skins. (Not all of the skins will come off, which is not a problem.) Add the hazelnuts, mango, and green onions to the rice. Toss lightly to combine.

TO MAKE THE DRESSING: Whisk together the olive oil, lemon zest and juice, soy sauce, ginger, garlic, and sugar. Taste and adjust the seasoning. Pour the dressing over the rice mixture and toss to blend. Divide the rice mixture among 4 dinner plates. Cut the salmon crosswise into 4 pieces. Place a salmon fillet in the center, on top of the salad, and serve immediately.

Chopped Salad with Salmon, Hard-Cooked Eggs, Potatoes, Frisée, Radish, and Avocado

Suggested wine: Beaujolais; rosé

Texturally and visually, I love chopped salads. I like to see individual ingredients play off each other in color, crunch, and taste. This main-course salad has it all. The rich, garlic-infused pink salmon rests center stage, surrounded by complementary flavors and textures. The crisp and slightly bitter frisée (curly endive) contrasts with the earthy, sweet-tasting potatoes. Smooth and creamy chunks of avocado and egg are the soft parts next to dense, crisp bites of radish. The mustard dressing, with lots of pepper, pulls all the flavors together. My palate guides my fork around my plate going from one interesting bite to the next in happy amusement.

SERVES 4 TO 6

Dressing

¾ cup extra-virgin olive oil

¼ cup rice vinegar

2 teaspoons Dijon mustard

2 tablespoons chopped fresh flat-leaf parsley

1 teaspoon sugar

1¼ teaspoons kosher or sea salt

Freshly ground pepper

16 new red potatoes

1½ teaspoons kosher or sea salt

2 tablespoons olive oil

2 cloves garlic, minced

1 teaspoon chopped fresh thyme

Freshly ground pepper

1 center-cut salmon fillet (about 1½ pounds), skin and pin bones removed *(see page 32)*

1 small head frisée (about 8 ounces), torn into bite-sized pieces

4 hard-cooked eggs, coarsely chopped *(see Cook's Note, page 126)*

2 green onions, including green tops, thinly sliced into rounds

2 bunches radishes, trimmed and halved

2 firm but ripe Hass avocados, pitted, peeled, and cut into ½-inch chunks

CONTINUED

Chopped Salad with Salmon, Hard-Cooked Eggs, Potatoes, Frisée, Radish, and Avocado *continued*

TO MAKE THE DRESSING: In a small jar with a tight-fitting lid, combine the extra-virgin olive oil, vinegar, mustard, parsley, sugar, salt, and lots of pepper. (Several good grinds of pepper make the vinaigrette taste robust, a perfect complement to the potatoes.) Cover tightly and shake vigorously to blend. Taste and adjust the seasoning. Set aside.

Fill a 3-quart saucepan two-thirds full of cold water, add the potatoes and 1 teaspoon of the salt, and bring to a simmer over medium-high heat. Cook, partially covered, just until tender, 18 to 20 minutes. Drain and let cool, then cut in half, keeping the skin on. Place in a medium bowl. Give the dressing a vigorous shake and toss the potatoes with about $1/4$ cup of the dressing. Set aside.

Meanwhile, preheat the oven to 400°F. In a small bowl, combine the olive oil, garlic, thyme, the remaining $1/2$ teaspoon salt, and a few grinds of pepper. Rub the salmon on all sides with this mixture. Place the salmon, skinned side down, in a baking dish and bake in the center of the oven for 14 to 20 minutes, depending on the thickness of the fish. The salmon is done when it appears almost opaque throughout, but still very moist, or an instant-read thermometer inserted in the center registers between 125° and 130°F. Remove the salmon and set aside to cool slightly.

Cut the salmon into 4 to 6 serving-sized pieces and place in the center of a large serving platter. Visually divide the rest of the platter into five wedge-shaped sections. Arrange the potatoes in one section, the frisée next to it, and the chopped eggs next to the frisée, scattering the green onions over the eggs and potatoes. Arrange the radishes next to the eggs. Place the chunks of avocado between the potatoes and the radishes. (This maximizes the lovely contrast of colors.) Give the remaining dressing another vigorous shake and drizzle it over everything except the potatoes. Grind a little pepper over the top and serve immediately.

COOK'S NOTE

To hard-cook an egg so that no green color coats the yolk, proceed as follows: Place the eggs in a small saucepan. Add cold water to cover by 1 inch and add a pinch of salt. Bring to a boil, and then immediately reduce the temperature to low; the water should barely simmer. Set a timer for 11 minutes. As soon as the timer goes off, pour off the boiling water and run cold water over the eggs until they are cool enough to handle. Peel under running water. If you're not using the eggs immediately, leave the shells on and refrigerate for up to 5 days. Write "HB" on the eggshells with a pencil to indicate they've been cooked.

Hot-Smoked Salmon Salad with Curly Endive and Bacon

Suggested wine: California or French chardonnay; Beaujolais; rosé

Once you have tried hot-smoking salmon, whether in a stovetop smoker, a wok, or on the grill, you'll wonder how a piece of fish with almost no embellishments can taste so good. This is great-tasting diet food! Assemble the salad while the salmon is smoking, and in 25 minutes you will have a fabulous main-course salad. A crusty loaf of bread is all you'll need.

SERVES 4

1 heaping tablespoon alder wood chips

Nonstick cooking spray

1 center-cut salmon fillet (about 1½ pounds), skin on and scaled, pin bones removed, skin dried by wiping with a knife *(see pages 30–33)*

Juice of ½ lemon

Freshly ground pepper

1 head curly endive (about 12 ounces), torn into bite-sized pieces

2 hard-cooked eggs, finely chopped *(see Cook's Note, facing page)*

3 strips cooked bacon, crumbled

6 tablespoons extra-virgin olive oil

1½ tablespoons cider vinegar

1 tablespoon heavy (whipping) cream

2 teaspoons Dijon mustard

1 teaspoon sugar

½ teaspoon kosher or sea salt

1 tablespoon chopped fresh tarragon

Using a stovetop smoker or wok, place the wood chips in a small pile in the center of the pan. Place a drip tray, covered with aluminum foil, on top of the chips. If using a wok, set a large sheet of aluminum foil loosely in place over the wood chips. Place a wire rack, sprayed with

CONTINUED

nonstick spray, on top of the drip tray or foil. Arrange the salmon on top, squeeze the lemon juice over the salmon, and sprinkle with freshly ground pepper. Slide the lid on the stovetop smoker or cover the wok, leaving it slightly open, and then place the smoker over medium heat. When the first wisp of smoke appears, close the lid. Smoke the salmon for 17 minutes. Turn the heat off and leave the salmon in the smoker, covered, for an additional 5 minutes.

WHILE THE SALMON IS SMOKING, MAKE THE SALAD: In a large bowl, toss together the endive, chopped eggs, and bacon. In a small bowl, whisk together the olive oil, vinegar, cream, mustard, sugar, salt, and pepper to taste. Add the tarragon and stir until combined.

When the salmon is done, give the dressing a final stir and toss with the salad. Arrange the salad on 4 dinner plates. Cut the salmon crosswise into 4 pieces and place a salmon fillet in the center, on top of the salad, and serve immediately.

MAIN COURSES

6

Whole Roast Salmon

Suggested wine: French red Burgundy; Oregon pinot noir

When you want drama for a dinner party, whether a sit-down affair or a buffet, nothing beats roasting an entire salmon and presenting it whole—especially if *you* caught the fish. Hooking a beauty from your favorite fishmonger—which most of us will be doing—is special, too. Here are a couple things to think about: measure your oven so you don't buy too large a salmon, *and* measure your largest rimmed baking sheet on the diagonal because that is how you will arrange the fish. If need be, you or the fishmonger can cut off the salmon's head. Hopefully, you won't need to cut off the tail, too, but that can be done to make it all work.

SERVES 8

Nonstick cooking spray
1 whole salmon (5 to 7 pounds), gutted, cleaned, and scaled, head
   and tail left on *(see pages 30–33)*
Kosher or sea salt
Freshly ground pepper
1 lemon, thinly sliced
1 yellow onion, thinly sliced
1 cup dry white wine
½ cup heavy (whipping) cream
2 tablespoons chopped fresh dill, plus dill sprigs for garnish

Preheat the oven to 400°F. Line a large rimmed baking sheet (11 by 17 inches) with aluminum foil. Spray the foil with nonstick cooking spray. Place the salmon on the pan, diagonally if necessary. If the fish is still too large, cut off the head using a sharp chef's knife. Tilt the fish on its back, open the cavity, and sprinkle with some salt and pepper. Lay the fish back on its side and arrange half the lemon slices along the length of the cavity. Overlap the onion slices on top, then place the remaining lemon slices on top of the onions. Using a ruler, measure the fish at its thickest part, usually right behind the head. Pour the wine over the fish and cover the fish completely with another piece of foil that has been sprayed with nonstick spray.

Place the pan in the oven and bake the fish for 10 minutes for every inch of thickness before checking for doneness. For example, if the salmon is 4 inches thick at its thickest point, then bake the fish for 40 minutes. Insert an instant-read thermometer into the thickest part, avoiding the spine; when it registers 125° to 130°F, the fish is done. (My preference is for the fish to be closer to 125°F, when it's moist and just beginning to flake.)

Remove the pan from the oven. Using two large spatulas, transfer the fish to a warmed large platter. (Alternatively, if you would rather carve the fish and serve individual plates instead of presenting the salmon whole, leave the fish in the pan.) If you transferred the salmon to a platter, cover the salmon loosely with aluminum foil while you make the sauce. If you left it in the pan, tilt the pan, using a spatula to restrain the fish, and pour the pan juices into a small saucepan. Cover the salmon if you left it in the pan. Add the cream to the pan juices and bring to a simmer over medium-high heat. Simmer and reduce until the sauce is thickened and coats the back of a spoon, about 3 minutes. Add the 2 tablespoons dill. Taste and add a little salt and pepper, if needed. Pour the sauce into a warmed small sauceboat for passing at the table or serving at the buffet.

To serve the fish whole, peel off the top skin or leave it on. (This decision is up to the chef—you either like salmon skin or you don't.) Using a carving knife, cut along the seam running lengthwise down the middle of the side of the fish, then make cuts crosswise into serving-sized portions. Using a knife and a serving spatula, loosen the pieces of fish. This will make it easier for your guests to serve themselves. When the top fillet has been served, lift off the backbone and ribs, then slide the onion and lemon slices to the side. Cut the bottom fillet into crosswise portions and serve.

If you are serving individual plates, follow the same procedure, portioning salmon onto each warmed plate. Spoon some sauce over the salmon or pass it at the table. Garnish with small sprigs of dill.

Whole Roast Salmon Stuffed with Bulgur Pilaf

Suggested wine: dolcetto; Valpolicella

Another dramatic presentation for entertaining is to roast a whole salmon stuffed with a savory bulgur pilaf. The bulgur can be cooked several hours or even a day ahead, then cooled and set aside or refrigerated until it is time to stuff the salmon. This will ease last-minute preparations for the cook. Accompany the salmon with a steamed or sautéed green vegetable—green beans, asparagus, Brussels sprouts, broccolini—and an easy and fabulous dinner party will be at hand. Have drinks and nibbles while the salmon bakes, or start with a soup or salad course.

SERVES 8

Bulgur Pilaf

3 tablespoons olive oil

1 large clove garlic, minced

1 yellow onion, chopped

½ cup pine nuts

1 red bell pepper, seeded, deribbed, and chopped

2 cups medium- or coarse-grind bulgur

2½ cups Salmon Stock *(page 77)* or canned low-sodium chicken broth

1 teaspoon kosher or sea salt

½ teaspoon freshly ground pepper

⅓ cup chopped fresh flat-leaf parsley, plus more for garnish

⅓ cup chopped fresh mint

1 whole salmon (5 to 7 pounds), gutted, cleaned, and scaled, head
   and tail left on *(see pages 30–33)*

Nonstick cooking spray

Juice of 1 lemon

½ cup dry white wine

TO MAKE THE BULGUR PILAF: In a 4-quart saucepan, heat the oil over medium heat. Swirl to coat the pan, then add the garlic and onion. Sauté, stirring frequently, until soft but not brown, about 4 minutes. Add the pine nuts and bell pepper and sauté until well coated with oil and the pepper softens slightly, 3 minutes longer. Add the bulgur and stir until well coated with oil. Immediately add the stock or broth, salt, and pepper. Bring to a boil, then reduce the heat to low, cover, and simmer until all the liquid has been absorbed, 8 to 10 minutes. Transfer to a mixing bowl. Stir in the parsley and mint and let cool to room temperature.

Meanwhile, preheat the oven to 400°F. Line a large rimmed baking sheet (11 by 17 inches) with aluminum foil. Spray the foil with nonstick cooking spray. Place the salmon on the pan, diagonally if necessary. If the fish is still too large, cut off the head using a sharp chef's knife. Squeeze the lemon juice all over the fish and then tilt the fish on its back, open the cavity, and squeeze lemon juice inside. Lay the fish back on its side and spoon the cooled bulgur pilaf along the length of the cavity, mounding it and allowing some to tumble out. Place any remaining pilaf in a buttered baking dish and heat separately. Pour the wine over the fish and cover the fish completely with another piece of foil that has been sprayed with nonstick spray.

Place the pan in the oven and bake the fish for 30 minutes. Remove the foil from the salmon and bake the fish 10 minutes longer. Insert an instant-read thermometer into the thickest part of the fish, avoiding the spine; when it registers 125° to 130°F, the fish is done. (My preference is for the fish to be closer to 125°F, when it's moist and just beginning to flake.)

Remove the pan from the oven and let the fish rest for 5 minutes. Using two large spatulas, transfer the fish to a warmed large platter. (Alternatively, if you would rather carve the fish and serve individual plates instead of presenting the salmon whole, leave the fish in the pan.) To serve the fish whole, peel off the top skin or leave it on. (This decision is up to the chef—you either like salmon skin or you don't.) Using a carving knife, cut along the seam running lengthwise down the middle of the side of the fish, then make cuts crosswise into serving-sized portions. Using a knife and serving spatula, loosen the pieces of fish. This will make it easier for your guests to serve themselves. When the top fillet has been served with generous spoonfuls of bulgur pilaf, spoon the remaining stuffing to the side so you can lift off the backbone and ribs. Cut the bottom fillet into crosswise portions and serve with the pilaf.

If you are serving individual plates, follow the same procedure, portioning salmon and pilaf onto each warmed plate. Garnish with chopped parsley.

Riesling-Poached Salmon

Suggested wine: riesling

A dieter's delight! Nothing could be simpler and tastier than a glorious fresh fillet of salmon poached in riesling. With the subtle spicing of star anise and peppercorns, a bit of exotic flavor is imparted, but it's the rich, full taste of the salmon that makes this entrée special. It is perfect either for an easy weeknight meal or a dinner for company. Serve the salmon with steamed asparagus, green beans, or sugar snap peas.

SERVES 4

2 cups dry riesling wine
½ cup water
2 star anise pods
10 peppercorns
4 to 6 thick salmon fillets (about 6 ounces each), skin and pin bones removed *(see pages 30–33)*
1 tablespoon extra-virgin olive oil
2 tablespoons chopped fresh cilantro
Kosher or sea salt
Freshly ground pepper

In a sauté pan just large enough to hold the salmon in a single layer, combine the wine, water, star anise, and peppercorns. Bring to a boil over medium heat, reduce the heat to low, and simmer for 5 minutes. Using a spatula, carefully slip the salmon into the pan, cover, and poach until almost opaque throughout, or an instant-read thermometer inserted in the center registers 125° to 130°F, about 8 minutes.

Transfer the salmon to warmed dinner plates or shallow pasta bowls. Drizzle each fillet with a little olive oil and sprinkle some chopped cilantro on top. Taste the poaching liquid and season lightly with salt and pepper. Spoon a couple of tablespoons of the poaching liquid around each fillet and serve immediately.

Austin's Soy-Lacquered Salmon with Green Onions

Suggested wine: Spanish albariño or Portuguese alvarinho; sauvignon blanc

My close friends Roxane and Austin Huang, now married, joke that they are together because Austin cooked this fabulous salmon dish for Roxane right after they had met. Austin learned to make this dish from his mother, Yoemin Liu, originally from West Lake in the city of Hanzhou about 250 miles from Shanghai. While most fish dishes in China are panfried and the sauce is added later, in this Shanghai-style recipe the fish is first poached in water and then finished in a flavorful broth. Austin's mother calls this recipe West Lake Sweet Vinegar Fish, but I'm giving Austin full credit because he has so generously shared this recipe with me.

SERVES 4

2 cups water

½ cup soy sauce

¼ cup distilled white vinegar

¼ cup sugar

6 green onions, including green tops

10 quarter-sized slices peeled fresh ginger

4 salmon fillets (about 6 ounces each), skin and pin bones removed *(see pages 30–33)*

Fill a 10-inch sauté pan with the water. Set aside. In a 2-cup liquid measuring cup or bowl, combine the soy sauce, vinegar, and sugar. Stir until the sugar dissolves. Cut 2 of the green onions into 1-inch lengths and add them to the water in the pan. Cut the remaining green onions into 1-inch lengths and add them to the soy mixture. Add 4 slices of ginger to the water in the pan. Julienne the remaining slices and then add them to the soy mixture. Set aside.

Place the pan over medium-high heat and bring the water to a boil. Add the salmon fillets, reduce the heat so the water just simmers, cover, and poach the salmon for 5 minutes. Carefully drain almost all the water from the pan, leaving about $^1/_4$ cup poaching broth in the pan. Remove the ginger slices and green onions. Return the pan to the heat and add the soy mixture. Bring to a simmer and continue to poach the salmon, uncovered, basting the fillets every minute or so until the fish is almost opaque throughout, or an instant-read thermometer inserted in the center registers 125° to 130°F, about 4 minutes longer. The sauce should have reduced and thickened a little.

Transfer the salmon to warmed dinner plates or shallow pasta bowls. Spoon some of the sauce, including the green onions and julienned ginger, around the salmon and serve immediately.

Slow-Roasted Salmon with Parsley-Garlic Sauce on a Bed of Mashed Potatoes

Suggested wine: Oregon pinot noir

Simply gorgeous on the plate, a glistening fillet of salmon sits atop a mound of buttery mashed potatoes surrounded by an emerald green herb-infused butter sauce. A novice cook can make this entrée and feel like a three-star chef serving it. The simple technique of blanching parsley and then puréeing it is the basis for a scrumptious, easy-to-make sauce. No need to worry about the sauce separating—it won't. If you make the sauce ahead, just set it aside and rewarm it just before serving. Freeze the extra parsley purée and use it to make this sauce, or add a little to vegetable soup, or swirl some into a seafood risotto.

SERVES 4

Kosher or sea salt

1 cup tightly packed fresh flat-leaf parsley leaves, plus 2 tablespoons minced fresh parsley

3 tablespoons water, plus ¼ cup

3 large russet potatoes (about 2 pounds total), peeled and quartered

4 salmon fillets (about 6 ounces each), skin and pin bones removed *(see pages 30–33)*

2 tablespoons olive oil

¼ teaspoon cayenne pepper

1 cup (2 sticks) unsalted butter

⅔ cup milk, warmed

Freshly ground pepper

1 teaspoon minced garlic

Fill a 2-quart saucepan two-thirds full of water and bring to a boil over high heat. Add 1 teaspoon of salt to the boiling water and then add the 1 cup parsley. Cook just until tender and bright green, about 1½ minutes. Drain the parsley in a sieve. Run cold water over the parsley until it is cool. Squeeze the parsley to remove the excess water. Place in a blender, add the 3 tablespoons water, and blend until puréed. Transfer to a small bowl and set aside.

CONTINUED

Slow-Roasted Salmon with Parsley-Garlic Sauce
on a Bed of Mashed Potatoes *continued*

Place the potatoes in a large saucepan and cover with cold water. Partially cover the pot and bring to a boil over high heat. Add 1 teaspoon of salt and reduce the heat so the water boils gently. Cook until the potatoes are tender when pierced with a knife, 12 to 15 minutes.

Meanwhile, preheat the oven to 250°F. Arrange the salmon on a rimmed baking sheet lined with parchment paper. Rub each fillet with olive oil and sprinkle lightly with a little salt and cayenne pepper. Set aside. Melt $1/2$ cup of the butter in a small sauté pan. Set aside and keep warm.

When the potatoes are tender, place the salmon in the oven to bake and set a timer for 20 minutes. Drain the potatoes in a colander. Using a ricer or potato masher, mash the potatoes. Stir the melted butter into the potatoes and then gradually add the milk. Beat until smooth and creamy. Add salt and pepper to taste. Cover and keep warm.

While the salmon is baking, bring the $1/4$ cup water to a boil in the sauté pan you used to melt the butter. Reduce the heat to low. Cut the remaining $1/2$ cup butter into 4 pieces and, using a whisk, stir the butter into the water a chunk at a time. Stir in 2 tablespoons of the parsley purée, the garlic, $1/4$ teaspoon of salt, and a couple of grinds of pepper. Taste and adjust the seasoning. Set aside and keep warm.

Check the salmon. The salmon is done when the fat between the layers begins to turn whitish and opaque and the fish flakes slightly. An instant-read thermometer inserted in the center should register 125° to 130°F. When salmon is cooked gently at such a low temperature the fish looks underdone because the color is so beautifully pink and vivid, but it is fully cooked.

To serve, place a portion of mashed potatoes in the center of warmed dinner plates or shallow pasta bowls. Top with a piece of salmon and drizzle some of the sauce around each plate. Garnish with a little minced parsley and serve immediately.

Slow-Roasted Salmon with Fennel and a White Wine–Herb Sauce

Suggested wine: French chardonnay

Don't be deterred from making this entrée because it requires you to make a reduced wine sauce—a beurre blanc. This recipe is knockout delicious and easy to make. With everything chopped and measured, this dish is finished in 20 minutes—the time it takes the salmon to cook. For company and relaxed entertaining, reduce the wine mixture up to 1 hour ahead, and have the salmon prepped and ready to bake, then all you'll need to do is stir the butter and herbs into the sauce just before serving. Start with a hearty salad or serve one after the entrée, offer a crusty baguette, add a simple dessert, and there's a perfect dinner party menu.

SERVES 4

4 salmon fillets (about 6 ounces each), skin and pin bones removed *(see pages 30–33)*

2 tablespoons olive oil

Kosher or sea salt

2 cups dry white wine

⅓ cup diced shallots

2 tablespoons fresh lemon juice

2 cups thinly sliced fennel bulb, plus ⅓ cup chopped fennel fronds

¾ cup (1½ sticks) unsalted butter, at room temperature, cut into 6 pieces

⅓ cup chopped fresh dill

⅓ cup snipped fresh chives

Preheat the oven to 250°F. Arrange the salmon on a rimmed baking sheet lined with parchment paper. Rub each fillet with olive oil and sprinkle lightly with a little salt. Place the salmon in the oven to bake and set a timer for 20 minutes.

WHILE THE SALMON IS BAKING, MAKE THE SAUCE: In a 4-quart saucepan over high heat, bring the wine, shallots, and lemon juice to a boil. Reduce the heat to medium-low and simmer

CONTINUED

the wine until reduced to 1$\frac{1}{4}$ cups, about 10 minutes. Add the sliced fennel and $\frac{1}{2}$ teaspoon salt and simmer until the fennel is crisp-tender, 5 minutes longer. Using a wooden spoon or heat-proof spatula, stir the butter into the wine mixture, a chunk at a time, until emulsified. Taste and adjust the seasoning. Set aside and keep warm.

Check the salmon. The salmon is done when the fat between the layers begins to turn whitish and opaque and the fish flakes slightly. An instant-read thermometer inserted in the center should register 125° to 130°F. When salmon is cooked gently at such a low temperature the fish looks underdone because the color is so beautifully pink and vivid, but it is fully cooked.

Just before serving, stir the fennel fronds, dill, and chives into the sauce. Place the salmon fillets in the center of warmed shallow pasta bowls. Spoon $\frac{1}{4}$ of the sauce, including $\frac{1}{4}$ of the fennel, over each salmon fillet and serve immediately.

Pan-Roasted Salmon with Brown Butter and Parsley

Suggested wine: French white Burgundy; California chardonnay

The first time I had a brown butter and parsley sauce was with seared scallops at the Cape Cod Room in Chicago. That was twenty years ago, but I've never forgotten the taste or preparation. The scallops were seared in butter over very high heat just until opaque. Here, I'm browning butter in one small pan and pan-roasting salmon in an ovenproof skillet, then pouring the butter sauce over the top. It's fabulous with a steamed vegetable such as broccoli or asparagus, but divine on a bed of mashed potatoes.

SERVES 4

4 center-cut salmon fillets (about 6 ounces each), skin on and scaled, pin bones removed,
  skin dried by wiping with a knife *(see pages 30–33)*
Kosher or sea salt
Freshly ground pepper
½ cup (1 stick) unsalted butter
2 tablespoons olive oil
4 teaspoons fresh lemon juice
2 tablespoons minced fresh flat-leaf parsley, plus more for garnish

Arrange an oven rack in the center of the oven and preheat the oven to 450°F. Season the salmon on all sides with salt and pepper to taste. Set aside.

In a small, heavy saucepan over medium heat, melt the butter. Let the butter cook until it turns a rich nut brown color, about 5 minutes. Watch carefully to keep it from burning. Set aside.

To pan-roast the salmon, in a large, heavy ovenproof skillet, preferably cast iron, heat the olive oil over high heat until almost smoking. Swirl to coat the pan and then add the salmon, skin side down. Cook until the skin is browned and crisp, about 4 minutes. After about 3 minutes, shake the pan once to make sure the fillets aren't sticking. Carefully turn the fillets, then transfer the skillet to the oven and roast the salmon until just cooked through, about 4 minutes longer.

As soon as the salmon goes into the oven, rewarm the butter over medium heat. When hot, add the lemon juice, the 2 tablespoons parsley, ¼ teaspoon of salt, and a couple of grinds of pepper.

To serve, place a piece of salmon in the center of a warmed dinner plate. Top with a generous spoonful of browned butter. Garnish with some parsley and serve immediately.

Pan-Roasted Salmon with a Pomegranate and Fennel Salsa

Suggested wine: Spanish albariño or Portuguese alvarinho

I like to serve this in the fall when pomegranates and fennel are in abundance at the market. The salsa is beautiful and vibrant, with bright red seeds and green flecks of jalapeno, green onion, and cilantro set against the diced white fennel. The subtle kick of cayenne pepper dusted on top of the salmon partners perfectly with this crunchy, big-flavored salsa. This salsa would be great with grilled salmon, too.

SERVES 4

Salsa

1 large fennel bulb, trimmed (fronds reserved)

1 pomegranate

1 jalapeno chile, seeded, deribbed, and minced

2 green onions, including green tops, finely chopped

¼ cup chopped fresh cilantro

2 tablespoons extra-virgin olive oil

2 tablespoons fresh lime juice

1 teaspoon kosher or sea salt

½ teaspoon sugar

Freshly ground pepper

4 center-cut salmon fillets (about 6 ounces each), skin on and scaled, pin bones removed, skin dried by wiping with a knife *(see pages 30–33)*

Kosher or sea salt

Freshly ground pepper

¼ teaspoon cayenne pepper

2 tablespoons olive oil

TO MAKE THE SALSA: Cut the fennel bulb in half lengthwise, remove the core, and then cut the fennel into $1/4$-inch dice. Transfer to a medium bowl. Chop $1/4$ cup of the fronds, add 2 tablespoons to the bowl, and reserve the rest for garnish. To extract the pomegranate seeds, cut the fruit into quarters, and then break the seeds away from the pith using your fingertips. (I wear disposable surgical gloves that I buy at any pharmacy to keep my fingers from being stained red. I also extract the seeds underwater, placing a bowlful of water in the kitchen sink to contain any squirting pomegranate juice.) Transfer the pomegranate seeds to the bowl with the fennel. Add the jalapeno chile, green onions, cilantro, extra-virgin olive oil, lime juice, salt, sugar, and a few grinds of pepper. Taste and adjust the seasoning. Set aside until ready to serve. (The salsa can be made up to 1 day in advance. Cover and refrigerate. Remove from the refrigerator 45 minutes before serving to allow it to come to room temperature.)

To pan-roast the salmon, arrange an oven rack in the center of the oven and preheat the oven to 450°F. Season the salmon on all sides with a little salt and pepper, then dust the tops with the cayenne pepper. In a large, heavy ovenproof skillet, preferably cast iron, heat the olive oil over high heat until almost smoking. Swirl to coat the pan and then add the salmon, skin side down. Cook over high heat until the skin is browned and crisp, about 4 minutes. After about 3 minutes, shake the pan once to make sure the fillets aren't sticking. Carefully turn the fillets and then transfer the skillet to the oven and roast the salmon until almost opaque throughout, about 4 minutes longer.

To serve, place a piece of salmon in the center of a warmed dinner plate. Top with a little salsa and spoon more next to the fillet. Garnish with some fennel fronds and serve immediately.

Pan-Roasted Salmon with Green Beans, Yellow Pear Tomatoes, and Basil Oil

Suggested wine: French white Burgundy; Orvieto

This entrée is art on a plate. Brilliantly colored crisp sautéed green beans are paired with little yellow pear tomatoes, and served with a perfectly pan-roasted salmon fillet. The drizzle of basil oil over the top adds a top-restaurant-quality look and taste to the plate. Yes, the entrée requires last-minute cooking, but it is easy and quick. Pan-roasting is such a fabulous technique that, once mastered, will become part of your regular repertoire for cooking fish, chicken, pork, beef, and even root vegetables. A heavy ovenproof skillet, a good fan for ventilation, and thick oven mitts are all you need. Ever since I learned about pan-roasting, my cast-iron skillet has gotten a heavy workout.

SERVES 4

Basil Oil

12 leaves fresh basil

½ cup extra-virgin olive oil

¼ teaspoon kosher or sea salt

4 center-cut salmon fillets (about 6 ounces each), skin on and scaled, pin bones removed, skin dried by wiping with a knife *(see pages 30–33)*

Kosher or sea salt

Freshly ground pepper

4 tablespoons olive oil

12 ounces young green beans, preferably haricots verts or baby Blue Lakes

1 pint yellow pear tomatoes, or other cherry or grape tomatoes

TO MAKE THE BASIL OIL: Fill a small saucepan two-thirds full of water and bring to a boil over high heat. Fill a small bowl with about 2 cups of ice water. Add the basil leaves to the boiling water, use a slotted spoon to submerge them, and cook until they turn bright green, 10 seconds. Using the slotted spoon, transfer them to the ice water. As soon as the basil leaves are cold, about 30 seconds, lift them out and squeeze firmly in your hand to release all the water. Pull the leaves apart and transfer them to a blender or mini-chop food processor. Add the extra-virgin olive oil and salt and blend or process until puréed. Transfer to a small container and set aside. (The basil oil can be made up to 5 days in advance and refrigerated in a small jar with a tight-fitting lid. It can also be frozen for up to 1 month.)

To pan-roast the salmon, arrange an oven rack in the center of the oven and preheat the oven to 450°F. Have ready 2 large skillets: a large, heavy ovenproof skillet, preferably cast iron, for cooking the salmon, and a large skillet for sautéing the green beans. Season the salmon on all sides with a little salt and pepper. Heat 2 tablespoons of the olive oil in the ovenproof skillet over high heat until almost smoking. Swirl to coat the pan and then add the salmon, skin side down. Cook over high heat until the skin is browned and crisp, about 4 minutes. After about 3 minutes, shake the pan once to make sure the fillets aren't sticking. Carefully turn the fillets, then transfer the skillet to the oven and roast the salmon until the fish is almost opaque throughout, but still very moist, about 4 minutes longer.

As soon as the salmon goes into the oven, place the other skillet over high heat and add the remaining 2 tablespoons olive oil. Swirl to coat the pan and add the green beans. Sauté, stirring frequently, until the beans are bright green and crisp-tender, about 3 minutes. Add the tomatoes and a little salt and pepper, and sauté until the tomatoes are heated through, 1 minute. Add 3 tablespoons of the basil oil to the skillet, stir a couple of times, and then remove the pan from the heat.

To serve, divide the vegetables among 4 warmed dinner plates and place a piece of salmon on top. Spoon a little more basil oil over each piece of salmon and serve immediately.

Javanese Roasted Salmon with Sautéed Spinach

Suggested wine: Alsatian riesling

Inspired by an entrée I've had many times at the restaurant Saucebox, in Portland, Oregon, I've done my best to re-create the dish. On several occasions I've quizzed the wait staff as to what was in the spicy, almost sweet-and-sour sauce and have finally achieved what I consider the right balance of flavors. They serve this dish on a beautiful Asian-style square plate. The salmon and sauce glisten, the spinach is barely wilted and a brilliant green, and a small molded circle of rice is added to the plate. This may be a restaurant recipe, but the techniques are easy enough for a home cook.

SERVES 4

8 tablespoons (1 stick) unsalted butter

½ teaspoon red pepper flakes

1 clove garlic, minced

¼ cup packed golden brown sugar

3 tablespoons fresh lime juice

¼ cup soy sauce

1 teaspoon cornstarch dissolved in 1 teaspoon water

4 center-cut salmon fillets (about 6 ounces each), skin and pin bones removed *(see pages 30–33)*

Kosher or sea salt

Freshly ground pepper

10 ounces baby spinach leaves

Preheat the oven to 400°F. In a small saucepan, melt 4 tablespoons of the butter over medium-high heat. Add the red pepper flakes and garlic and stir until fragrant, about 1 minute. Add the sugar, lime juice, and soy sauce and bring to a boil. Simmer, stirring frequently, until the sugar is dissolved and the mixture reduces slightly, about 3 minutes. Add the cornstarch mixture and boil until thick, about 1 minute. Set aside.

Have ready 2 large sauté pans and a rimmed baking sheet. Sprinkle the salmon lightly with a little salt and pepper. In one of the sauté pans, melt 2 tablespoons of the remaining butter over high heat. Swirl to coat the pan and add the salmon. Sear the salmon until golden on one side, about 2 minutes. Turn and sear the other side, about 2 minutes longer. Transfer the salmon to the baking sheet and spoon about 1 tablespoon of sauce over each fillet. Place in the oven and roast until the salmon is almost opaque throughout, about 5 minutes.

Meanwhile, melt the remaining 2 tablespoons butter in the other sauté pan over medium-high heat. Swirl to coat the pan and add the spinach. Using tongs, toss the spinach until wilted but still bright green, about 3 minutes. Season lightly with salt and pepper. Rewarm the sauce.

To serve, divide the spinach among 4 warmed dinner plates. Top each with a salmon fillet and drizzle each fillet with some of the sauce. Serve immediately. (Alternatively, serve the salmon on a bed of Japanese-style white rice accompanied with the spinach.)

Honey-Soy Broiled Salmon

Suggested wine: Washington State semillon; Oregon riesling

Gary Lopiccolo, a cooking enthusiast par excellence, sent me this recipe. I met Gary when I was teaching a cooking class in Los Gatos and he was my lead assistant. We immediately hit it off and talked food and cooking techniques while prepping for my class. He promised to assist me anytime I returned to teach in Los Gatos, and indeed he has. When I started writing this book, he sent me two recipes to try, referring to them as "amazing salmon dishes." This is one of them, and I wholeheartedly agree—this recipe is dynamite! It's great served with Japanese-style white rice and a steamed or sautéed vegetable such as baby bok choy or asparagus.

SERVES 4

4 center-cut salmon fillets (about 6 ounces each), skin on and scaled,
   pin bones removed *(see pages 30–33)*
2 tablespoons soy sauce
¼ cup rice vinegar
½ cup mirin *(see Cook's Notes, page 51)*
1 teaspoon peeled and finely grated fresh ginger

Sauce
4 teaspoons wasabi powder
2 tablespoons fresh lime juice
¼ cup soy sauce
½ cup honey

Steamed white rice for serving *(optional)*

To marinate the salmon, place the fillets in a baking dish just large enough to hold the salmon in a single layer. (Alternatively, you can place the salmon in a lock-top plastic freezer bag.) In a small bowl, combine the soy sauce, vinegar, mirin, and ginger. Pour over the fillets, turning to coat all sides. Marinate the salmon at room temperature for at least 30 minutes but no more than 1 hour. (If you leave the fish in the marinade for more than an hour, the acid in the marinade will begin to "cook" the fish.)

JUST BEFORE BROILING THE FISH, MAKE THE SAUCE: In a small saucepan, mix together the wasabi powder, lime juice, soy sauce, and honey. Place the pan over medium heat and bring the sauce to a boil, stirring constantly. Turn the heat to low and simmer, stirring constantly, until the sauce thickens and turns syrupy, about 2 minutes. Set aside and keep warm.

Arrange an oven rack or broiler pan about 3 to 4 inches from the heat source and preheat the broiler. Remove the salmon from the marinade, wiping off any excess marinade. Place the salmon on a baking sheet, skin side down, and broil until it begins to color, 3 to 4 minutes. Turn the salmon and cook, skin side up, until almost opaque throughout, but still very moist, about 3 minutes longer. (Don't worry if the skin starts to char; it will be removed before serving.)

To serve, have ready 4 warmed dinner plates. If serving the salmon over rice, arrange some rice in the center of each plate. Remove the skin from the salmon fillets, turn the fillets flesh side up, and arrange on the bed of rice. Drizzle some sauce over the top and serve immediately.

Josie's Favorite: Pan-Grilled Salmon on Braised Leeks with Parmigiano-Reggiano

Suggested wine: pinot grigio; Soave

This is the second recipe that Gary Lopiccolo sent me, with a sweet story to go along. We call the recipe Josie's Favorite in honor of his recently deceased mother, Josephine Marie Lopiccolo. At the funeral, all the relatives talked about her wonderful cooking and how everyone was going to miss it. Gary described his mother as "the stereotypical little Italian mom" who learned to cook from her mother-in-law, a legend in the kitchen, mostly because she wanted to impress her husband and prove herself to his mother. Gary cooked alongside his mother to learn her ways. When Gary made this salmon recipe for his mom, she told him, "I love this! Make it again soon. I'm practically licking my plate."

SERVES 4

4 tablespoons (½ stick) unsalted butter

6 leeks, white and light green parts only, halved lengthwise, rinsed, and cut into ½-inch slices

2 cups low-sodium chicken broth

Kosher or sea salt

Freshly ground pepper

4 center-cut salmon fillets (about 6 ounces each), skin on and scaled, pin bones removed, skin dried by wiping with a knife *(see pages 30–33)*

2 tablespoons olive oil

¾ cup freshly grated Parmigiano-Reggiano cheese

In a 10-inch sauté pan, melt the butter over medium heat and swirl to coat the pan. Add the leeks and sauté, stirring frequently, until they just begin to brown, 8 to 10 minutes. (Reduce the heat to low if the leeks begin to darken and get crisp at the edges.) Add the broth, stir to combine, and bring to a simmer. Adjust the heat so the broth is barely at a simmer, partially cover the pan, and cook, stirring occasionally, until the liquid is reduced and the leeks are very tender, 35 to 45 minutes. (The leeks should be very moist but not soupy at all.) Uncover and raise the heat to reduce the liquid, if necessary. Add salt and pepper to taste. Cover and keep warm.

To pan-grill the salmon, rub it on all sides with olive oil and sprinkle lightly with salt and pepper. Heat a large grill pan, preferably cast iron, over high heat until almost smoking. Add the salmon, skin side up, and sear on one side until beautiful grill marks are etched across the fillets, about 4 minutes. (If desired, after 3 minutes, turn the fillets a quarter turn, still skin side up, to create crosshatch marks.) Turn the fillets, skin side down, and cook until the salmon is almost opaque throughout, but still very moist, or an instant-read thermometer inserted in the center registers between 125° and 130°F, about 4 minutes longer.

To serve, place a portion of braised leeks in the center of 4 warmed dinner plates or shallow pasta bowls. Top with a piece of salmon and scatter a generous amount of the Parmesan over the salmon and leeks. Serve immediately. (It will seem like an overly generous amount of Parmesan to scatter over the top, but it's perfect and utterly delicious.)

Grilled Salmon Brochettes with Mango-Orange-Habanero Mojo

Suggested wine: Spanish albariño or Portuguese alvarinho

One look and one taste of this entrée and you know you've made a winner. An herb, garlic, and ginger marinade slicks the salmon, making every tender bite a fusion of flavor. This mojo is big, bright, and spiced—a vibrant orange-glow sauce that is deliriously delicious, punctuated with cilantro, and power-surged with habanero chile. If you and your friends can take the heat, use a whole habanero; half is plenty for me.

This recipe could easily be doubled or tripled for a big backyard party. Serve the skewers accompanied with rice, or a citrus-infused couscous, or on a bed of noodles.

SERVES 4

Marinade

½ cup extra-virgin olive oil

2 tablespoons Asian sesame oil

¼ cup minced fresh cilantro

2 large cloves garlic, minced

1 tablespoon peeled and minced fresh ginger

1 center-cut salmon fillet (about 2 pounds), skin and pin bones removed (*see pages 30–33*), cut into 1¼-inch cubes

Eight 10-inch bamboo skewers

Mango-Orange-Habanero Mojo

2 tablespoons rice vinegar

½ teaspoon ground cumin

½ teaspoon kosher or sea salt

1 ripe mango, peeled, pitted, and cut into large chunks

⅓ cup fresh orange juice

½ habanero or Scotch bonnet chile (or more to taste), seeded, deribbed, and coarsely chopped

2 tablespoons chopped fresh cilantro

CONTINUED

Grilled Salmon Brochettes with Mango-Orange-Habanero Mojo *continued*

2 red bell peppers, seeded, deribbed, and cut into 1-inch squares (about 32 pieces)
4 green onions, including green tops, cut into 1-inch lengths (about 32 pieces)
Kosher or sea salt
Vegetable oil for brushing

TO MAKE THE MARINADE: In a medium bowl, combine the olive oil, sesame oil, cilantro, garlic, and ginger. Stir well to blend. Add the salmon cubes and toss gently to coat on all sides with the marinade. Cover and set aside at room temperature for up to 45 minutes. (The salmon can be covered and refrigerated for up to 2 hours. Remove from the refrigerator 30 minutes before grilling.) Soak the bamboo skewers in water for at least 30 minutes, then drain.

Prepare a medium-hot fire in a charcoal grill or preheat a gas grill to medium-high.

TO MAKE THE MOJO: Combine the rice vinegar, cumin, and salt in a measuring cup and stir to dissolve the salt. In a blender, combine the mango, orange juice, and chile; blend until puréed. Blend in the rice vinegar mixture. Taste and add more chile, if desired. Add the cilantro and blend, with a quick on and off, just until mixed through. Transfer to a bowl or sauceboat and set aside.

To assemble the skewers, thread a cube of salmon, followed by a piece of red pepper and green onion, on a skewer. Repeat the process 3 more times. Repeat with the remaining 7 skewers. Season each skewer with a little salt, rotating to season evenly.

When ready to grill, brush the grill grate with vegetable oil. Place the skewers directly over the medium-hot fire. Cover the grill and cook on one side, about 4 minutes. Turn and cover again. Cook about 4 minutes longer, or until the salmon is almost opaque throughout, but still very moist.

To serve, have ready 4 warmed dinner plates. If serving the skewers over rice, arrange some rice in the center of each plate and place 2 skewers on top. Drizzle some of the mojo over the top and around the perimeter of each plate. Serve immediately. Pass the extra mojo at the table.

Grilled Salmon with a Pineapple-Habanero Salsa

Suggested wine: riesling; Spanish albariño or Portuguese alvarinho

This colorful, deliciously hot salsa is a perfect partner for grilled salmon. The smoky flavors and crisp, slightly charred edges of the salmon complement this tropical salsa. Habanero chiles are the hottest of the hot; 1 teaspoon of minced chile was enough for me in this recipe, but add more if you like. Get yourself some disposable surgical gloves at the pharmacy and wear them when working with chiles. It will keep the chile oils from penetrating and irritating your skin.

SERVES 4

Pineapple-Habanero Salsa

½ pineapple, peeled, halved lengthwise, cored, and cut into ¼-inch dice

1 small red bell pepper, seeded, deribbed, and cut into ¼-inch dice

2 green onions, including green tops, cut into ¼-inch dice

1 to 2 teaspoons minced habanero chile

2 tablespoons fresh lime juice

1 tablespoon packed light brown sugar

1 teaspoon chopped fresh thyme

½ teaspoon kosher or sea salt

4 salmon fillets (about 6 ounces each), skin on and scaled, pin bones removed,
 skin dried by wiping with a knife *(see pages 30–33)*

2 tablespoons olive oil

Kosher or sea salt

Freshly ground pepper

Vegetable oil for brushing

CONTINUED

TO MAKE THE SALSA: In a medium bowl, combine the pineapple, bell pepper, green onions, habanero chile, lime juice, sugar, thyme, and salt. Stir to combine. Cover and set aside for 1 hour before serving to allow the flavors to meld. (The salsa can be made up to 8 hours in advance. Cover and refrigerate. Remove from the refrigerator 45 minutes before serving.)

Prepare a medium-hot fire in a charcoal grill or preheat a gas grill to medium-high. Rub the salmon fillets with olive oil and sprinkle lightly with salt and pepper on all sides.

When ready to grill, brush the grill grate with vegetable oil. Place the salmon, skin side up, directly over the medium-hot fire. Cover the grill and cook on one side until beautiful grill marks are etched across the fillets, about 4 minutes. Turn and cover again. Cook until the salmon is almost opaque throughout, but still very moist, or an instant-read thermometer inserted in the center registers between 125° and 130°F, about 5 minutes more. Serve immediately, with a large spoonful of salsa to one side of each fillet.

Cedar-Planked Grilled Salmon

Suggested wine: Oregon pinot noir; gamay; aged Rioja

Grilling salmon on a plank of wood imparts a sweet and smoky, slightly charred flavor to the fish. The possibilities for flavor depend on the type of wood used—either cedar, alder, or oak—and the sauce, marinade, or rub chosen. This recipe gives you the basics along with a delicious combination: herb-rubbed salmon grilled on a cedar plank.

For hundreds of years, Native Americans living in the Pacific Northwest have cooked fish, in particular salmon, by planking it. A huge fire pit was built, sides of salmon were skewered or attached to the planks, and the bottom of the planks were driven into the ground so the salmon could grill-roast vertically, very slowly, next to the fire. The technique I describe here is much simpler!

SERVES 6 TO 8

1 untreated cedar plank, measuring about 15 by 7 by ⅜ inches *(see Cook's Notes, page 160)*
1 whole side of salmon (about 3 pounds), skin on and scaled, pin bones removed,
  skin dried by wiping with a knife *(see pages 30–33)*
Olive oil for brushing
Kosher or sea salt
Freshly ground pepper
Leaves from 4 sprigs fresh thyme
Leaves from 4 sprigs fresh rosemary
Juice of ½ lemon

Prepare a medium fire in a charcoal grill or preheat a gas grill to medium.

Meanwhile, rinse the cedar plank and place it in a pan, sink, or large leak-proof plastic bag filled with water. Soak the plank for about 20 minutes.

Rub the salmon with olive oil and sprinkle lightly with salt and pepper on all sides. Scatter the thyme and rosemary leaves over the flesh, pressing them lightly to help adhere to the flesh. Set aside.

CONTINUED

When ready to grill, place the soaked plank on the grill grate directly over the fire and close the lid. After a few minutes, the plank will begin to smoke and crackle. Turn the plank over and "toast" the other side for about 2 minutes. Uncover the grill, transfer the salmon fillet to the plank, and then cover the grill. Grill-smoke the salmon skin side down until the salmon is almost opaque throughout, but still very moist, or an instant-read thermometer inserted in the center registers between 125° and 130°F, 15 to 25 minutes, depending on the thickness of the fillet. (Keep a spray bottle with water nearby just in case the plank gets too hot and begins to flame. Extinguish the flame and continue grilling the salmon, adjusting the heat level of the grill if necessary.) Using 2 long spatulas, transfer the salmon to a warmed platter. Use tongs, heatproof gloves, or the spatulas to remove the plank from the heat. Set aside to cool. Squeeze lemon juice over the salmon, cut into individual servings, and serve immediately.

COOK'S NOTES

Untreated cedar or alder planks can be purchased from lumberyards or hardware stores. Have them cut to size or cut them yourself. A simpler, though slightly more expensive, approach is to buy precut planks specifically for grilling or baking salmon. Gourmet cooking stores carry them, or they can be ordered from Chinook Planks online at chinookplanks.com, or by calling 1-800-765-4408. • Cedar planks can be reused if they aren't too charred or cracked. Once the plank has cooled, brush it clean with a grill brush, set it upright to dry, and then store it in a brown paper bag. Resoak it before using.

Cheryl's Grill-Roasted Whole Salmon Stuffed with Fresh Dill and Lemon

Suggested wine: Oregon pinot noir; French chardonnay

In the summer, I love to serve a sizzling whole grilled salmon on a large platter surrounded by grilled vegetables. My dear friend and assistant, Cheryl Russell, shared this recipe with me. We both agree that grilling a whole salmon in a grill basket is the surefire way to achieve a beautifully crisp-skinned, moist fish that doesn't stick to the grill. My favorite style of grill basket is a large fish-shaped grill cage. Though they come in different sizes, I prefer a large one because I'm usually grilling a 5- to- 7-pound sockeye salmon. These metal cages are hinged on one end and have wire handles on the other end that clasp together when the basket is closed. They have metal feet on both sides so the basket sits up off the grill grate. If you oil the skin of the fish and spray the grill basket, you'll be able to remove the fish without the skin tearing. This grill basket works equally well for grilling a whole side of salmon.

SERVES 8

Nonstick cooking spray
1 whole salmon (5 to 7 pounds), preferably sockeye, gutted, cleaned, and scaled,
　head removed and tail on, skin dried by wiping with a knife *(see pages 30–33)*
Kosher or sea salt
Freshly ground pepper
16 sprigs fresh dill, plus more for garnish
1 very small onion, thinly sliced
1 lemon, cut into paper-thin rounds
Olive oil for brushing

Prepare a medium fire in a charcoal grill or preheat a gas grill to medium. Have ready a large fish-shaped grill basket. Spray the grill basket with nonstick cooking spray. Before stuffing the cavity of the salmon, check to see if the salmon will fit comfortably, albeit snuggly, in the grill basket. Trim off the tail if the salmon is too long for the basket.

Sprinkle the cavity of the salmon with salt and pepper. Lay 3 sprigs of dill down the length of the cavity. Overlap the onion slices on top of the dill. Overlap slices of lemon on top of the onion, then lay 3 more small sprigs of dill on top. Brush or rub the skin of the salmon all over with olive oil and sprinkle lightly with salt and pepper. Place 5 sprigs of dill along the length of the bottom side of the grill basket and arrange the salmon on top. Place the remaining 5 sprigs of dill on top, along the length of the salmon. Securely close the basket.

To grill the salmon, the temperature of the grill should be about 425°F. Move coals to the side, or adjust the temperature of a gas grill, to attain a moderate internal temperature when the grill is covered. Place the grill basket on the grill grate and cover the grill. Grill the salmon on one side until the skin is crisp and brown, about 10 minutes. Turn the basket over and grill the fish on the other side until the salmon is almost opaque throughout, but still very moist, or an instant-read thermometer inserted in the center registers between 125° and 130°F, about 8 minutes longer.

To serve, unlatch the grill basket slowly to avoid tearing the skin. Use a table knife to release any skin sticking to the wires. Remove the dill from both sides of the salmon and discard. Carefully lift and transfer the salmon to a warmed serving platter. Using a carving knife, cut along the seam running lengthwise down the middle of the side of the fish. Then make cuts crosswise into serving-sized portions. Using a knife and serving spatula, loosen the pieces of fish. This will make it easier for your guests to serve themselves. When the top fillet has been served, lift off the backbone and ribs, then slide the onion and lemon slices to the side. Cut the bottom fillet into crosswise portions and serve.

If you are serving individual plates, follow the same procedure, portioning salmon onto each warmed plate. Garnish with small sprigs of dill.

Hot–Smoked Salmon with Bagels, Herbed Cream Cheese, and Red Onions **166** • *Smoked Salmon Blintzes* **168** •

Salmon Hash **171** • *Salmon, Chanterelle, and Shallot Omelet* **172** • *Smoked Salmon Frittata with Onions,*

Potatoes, and Herbs **174** • *Roasted Leek and Salmon Tartlets* **176** • *Poached Eggs on Grilled Olive Bread*

with Smoked Salmon **180** • *Spring Vegetable Potpie with Salmon* **182** • *Smoked Salmon, Onion,*

and Arugula Quiche **185**

BRUNCH AND LUNCH

7

Hot-Smoked Salmon with Bagels, Herbed Cream Cheese, and Red Onions

Suggested wine or beverage: Champagne; domestic sparkling wine; Bloody Mary

As a delicious alternative to the classic lox and bagels with cream cheese, I've put together an unbelievably good open-faced bagel sandwich. Fluffy herb-flecked cream cheese, with a hit of lemon zest and a few capers thrown in for good taste, is smeared on toasted bagel halves. A scattering of red onion packs a flavor punch and is topped with smoky alder-scented salmon. This recipe allots a whole bagel per person; lighter eaters might only want a half.

SERVES 4

1 heaping tablespoon alder wood chips

Nonstick cooking spray

1 center-cut salmon fillet (about 1 pound), skin on, pin bones removed *(see pages 30–33)*

1 tablespoon olive oil

Freshly ground pepper

Herbed Cream Cheese *(recipe follows)*

4 bagels, halved and toasted

1 red onion, sliced into paper-thin rounds

Using a stovetop smoker or wok, place the wood chips in a small pile in the center of the pan. Place a drip tray, covered with aluminum foil, on top of the chips. If using a wok, set a large sheet of aluminum foil loosely in place over the wood chips. Place a wire rack, sprayed with nonstick spray, on top of the drip tray or foil. Arrange the salmon on top. Rub the salmon with the olive oil, then sprinkle with a little pepper. Slide the lid on the stovetop smoker or cover the wok, leaving it slightly open, then place the smoker over medium heat. When the first wisp of smoke appears, close the lid. Smoke the salmon for 17 minutes. Turn the heat off and leave the salmon in the smoker, covered, for an additional 5 minutes. Transfer the salmon to a cutting board. Slide a spatula between the salmon flesh and the skin. Discard the skin, cut the salmon into large chunks, and arrange on a serving plate.

While the salmon is smoking, make the herbed cream cheese.

To serve, arrange the onion slices on a serving plate, place the toasted bagels in a basket, and pass everything at the table. Allow your guests to smear a bagel half with the herbed cream cheese, place some onion on top, and arrange chunks of salmon over the onion.

HERBED CREAM CHEESE

1 package (8 ounces) cream cheese, at room temperature

¼ cup snipped fresh chives

2 tablespoons minced fresh flat-leaf parsley

2 tablespoons chopped fresh dill

1 tablespoon capers, rinsed and drained

2 teaspoons grated lemon zest

½ teaspoon freshly ground pepper

In a food processor fitted with the metal blade, process the cream cheese until smooth and softened. Scatter the chives, parsley, dill, capers, lemon zest, and pepper over the cream cheese. Pulse to combine, scraping down the sides of the work bowl as needed. Transfer to a serving bowl. (The herbed cream cheese can be made up to 2 days in advance. Cover and refrigerate. Remove from the refrigerator 45 minutes before serving.)

Smoked Salmon Blintzes

Suggested wine: Champagne; domestic sparkling wine; Beaujolais; rosé

Blintzes are traditionally stuffed with sweetened cheese and a hint of sweet spices, but for a twist here's a savory crêpe beautifully flecked with green chives. Though the filling uses two different styles of cottage cheese, the addition of lemon, pepper, chives, and diced lox turns these into an ultimate brunch entrée. They taste as great as they look. For easy entertaining, make these several weeks ahead and freeze them. Thaw the blintzes overnight in the refrigerator, and they are ready to brown and serve.

MAKES 24 BLINTZES; SERVES 8 TO 12

Crêpe Batter

1½ cups all-purpose flour

1½ teaspoons kosher or sea salt

2 teaspoons baking powder

Freshly ground white pepper

4 large eggs, lightly beaten

1⅓ cups milk

1 cup water

3 tablespoons snipped fresh chives

Filling

16 ounces dry-curd cottage cheese

16 ounces small-curd cottage cheese

3 large egg yolks

Grated zest of 1 lemon

Freshly ground white pepper

2 tablespoons snipped fresh chives

8 ounces thinly sliced smoked salmon (lox), diced

4 tablespoons vegetable oil

3 tablespoons unsalted butter

1½ cups sour cream for garnish

3 tablespoons snipped fresh chives for garnish

CONTINUED

Smoked Salmon Blintzes *continued*

TO MAKE THE CRÊPE BATTER: Sift together the flour, salt, baking powder, and a few grinds of pepper. Whisk in the eggs and milk, then add the water, whisking to make a smooth batter. Stir in the chives. Set the batter aside to rest for 30 minutes.

WHILE THE BATTER IS RESTING, MAKE THE FILLING: In a food processor fitted with the metal blade, combine the two types of cottage cheese, the egg yolks, lemon zest, and a few grinds of pepper. Process until combined, about 1 minute. Transfer to a bowl and stir in the chives and salmon. Cover and refrigerate.

To make the crêpes, heat a 6-inch crêpe pan or skillet, preferably nonstick, over medium heat. Using a pastry brush or paper towel folded into a small square, oil the pan lightly without leaving a pool of oil. Stir the batter each time you make a crêpe to distribute the chives. Pour about 3 tablespoons of batter into the pan and tip and tilt the pan to spread the batter evenly. Cook until the crêpe is lightly browned on the bottom, about 1 minute. Turn the crêpe and cook on the other side for 30 seconds. Slide the crêpe onto a plate to cool. Repeat the process to make 24 crêpes, coating the skillet with oil as needed. Stack the crêpes as they are cooked.

To assemble the blintzes, place $1/4$ cup filling on the bottom third of each crêpe. Fold up envelope style by first folding the bottom over the filling, then folding in the two sides. Finish rolling the blintz so the seam is on the bottom. (The blintzes can be made up to this point, covered, and refrigerated for up to 1 day or frozen up to 1 month. Thaw in the refrigerator overnight.)

Preheat the oven to 200°F. In a 10- or 12-inch skillet, melt 1 tablespoon butter with 1 tablespoon oil over medium heat, then swirl to coat the pan. Add as many blintzes, seam side up, as will fit in the pan without crowding. Cook until nicely browned on one side, about 2 minutes. Turn and cook until nicely browned on the other side, about 2 minutes longer. Transfer to a baking sheet and keep warm in the oven while browning additional batches. Add more butter and oil to the pan for each batch.

When ready to serve, stir the sour cream until smooth and creamy. Arrange 2 or 3 blintzes in the center of each warmed plate, spoon a little sour cream over them, and garnish with chives.

Salmon Hash

Suggested wine: dolcetto; Valpolicella

There is no better or more enjoyable way to use up leftover salmon than to make salmon hash. This hash is wonderful for Sunday brunch, or for a weeknight supper served with a tossed green salad or a simple steamed vegetable and a crusty loaf of bread. I have a habit of cooking "big," intentionally planning for great leftovers. For this dish, I would most likely have roasted or grilled a whole salmon, about 7 pounds including the head, and then served my family of four a little over half of the fish. That leaves just shy of 4 cups of salmon to make hash—perfect!

SERVES 4

4 tablespoons (½ stick) unsalted butter

2 pounds red-skinned, Yukon Gold, or Yellow Finn potatoes, peeled and cut into ½-inch dice

1 large yellow onion, cut into ½-inch dice

2 celery stalks, halved lengthwise, then cut crosswise into ½-inch-thick slices

1 tablespoon chopped fresh dill

2 teaspoons minced fresh thyme

1 teaspoon kosher or sea salt

½ teaspoon freshly ground pepper

3½ cups coarsely flaked roasted or grilled salmon

1 cup chopped fresh flat-leaf parsley

In a 12-inch skillet or sauté pan, preferably cast iron, melt the butter over medium heat and swirl to coat the pan. Add the potatoes and onion and sauté until just coated with butter, about 1 minute. Cover and cook for 7 minutes to steam the potatoes. Add the celery, stir briefly, then cover and cook 3 minutes longer. Uncover the pan, increase the heat to medium-high, and add the dill, thyme, salt, and pepper. Cook, stirring frequently, until the potatoes are lightly browned, 20 to 25 minutes. Add the salmon and parsley and cook just until the salmon is heated through. Use a heatproof rubber spatula to stir the salmon so the salmon pieces don't fall apart. Taste and adjust the seasoning. Serve immediately.

Salmon, Chanterelle, and Shallot Omelet

Suggested wine: French red Burgundy; Meursault

As a brunch dish or Sunday night supper, nothing is more satisfying than a properly made omelet: creamy in the center, lightly browned on the outside, and, in this recipe, stuffed with an earthy, herb-scented wild mushroom filling accented with slices of smoked salmon.

I like to use an 8-inch frying pan for making a three-egg omelet. A 7-inch pan works better for a two-egg version. Purists may prefer a seasoned steel or aluminum omelet pan, but I find it easier to use a nonstick pan. With a little experience and two identically sized pans, you can whip out two omelets at once and feel like a real short-order cook! Make sure to have your dinner plates warmed so the omelet stays hot.

SERVES 2

2 tablespoons olive oil

1 large shallot, thinly sliced

6 ounces chanterelle mushrooms, wiped clean and very coarsely chopped

1 teaspoon minced fresh thyme

1½ tablespoons minced fresh flat-leaf parsley

¾ teaspoon kosher or sea salt

Freshly ground pepper

6 large eggs, at room temperature

2 tablespoons crème fraîche or sour cream

4 teaspoons unsalted butter, at room temperature

2 ounces thinly sliced smoked salmon (lox), cut into 1-inch pieces

In a 10-inch sauté pan heat the olive oil over medium heat, and swirl to coat the pan. Add the shallot and sauté, stirring constantly, until softened, 1 minute. Add the mushrooms and sauté, stirring frequently, until just beginning to soften and brown at the edges, about 4 minutes. Add the thyme, parsley, ¼ teaspoon of the salt, and a few grinds of pepper. Sauté for 1 minute longer and then remove from the heat. Keep warm.

Break 3 eggs into each of 2 small bowls. Place 1 tablespoon crème fraîche or sour cream in each bowl. Add $1/4$ teaspoon of salt and a couple grinds of pepper to each bowl. Using a fork, beat the eggs until fluffy.

Place 2 teaspoons of the butter in an 8-inch frying pan, preferably nonstick. Melt the butter over medium-high heat and swirl to coat the pan. Add the eggs from one bowl and allow them to coagulate on the bottom of the pan for a few seconds, then give the eggs a quick stir with a fork or a heatproof rubber spatula. Allow a new "skin" to form on the bottom. Tilt the pan, lifting the omelet at the edges to allow some of the uncooked egg to run underneath. Jerk the pan a little to make sure the omelet isn't sticking. When the omelet is nicely formed and the eggs are cooked but still very soft, spoon half of the mushroom mixture on the half of the omelet farthest from the handle and lay half the pieces of salmon on top. Use your spatula to fold the other half of the omelet over the filling, then slide the omelet onto a warm plate. Keep warm while you make the second omelet. Serve immediately once the second omelet is made. (Make both omelets at once if you have two identical pans.)

Smoked Salmon Frittata with Onions, Potatoes, and Herbs

Suggested wine: Chianti

You don't need to master a quick flick-of-the-wrist technique or fret over last-minute timing when making frittatas; they're forgiving and easy. Frittatas are open-faced Italian omelets that are skillet-cooked and usually finished under the broiler. Making frittatas for brunch or lunch is a snap when you have a number of people to feed, but don't overlook them for an easy week-night meal. I like to serve this frittata with a green salad and some crusty bread. For brunch, add some sliced fruit and a coffee cake, and you're set.

SERVES 6 TO 8

3 tablespoons olive oil
1 onion, cut into ½-inch dice
12 ounces red-skinned potatoes, peeled and cut into ½-inch dice
12 large eggs
½ cup milk
¼ cup chopped fresh flat-leaf parsley
¼ cup chopped fresh dill
1 teaspoon kosher or sea salt
Freshly ground pepper
8 ounces alder-smoked or other hot-smoked salmon (*see page 124*), skin removed,
   and flaked into bite-sized pieces

In a 12-inch ovenproof skillet, preferably nonstick, heat the olive oil over medium heat. Swirl to coat the pan, then add the onion and potatoes. Sauté, stirring occasionally, until the onion softens, about 4 minutes. Turn the heat to medium-low, cover the pan, and cook the onion mixture, stirring occasionally, until the onion and potatoes are tender and beginning to brown, about 10 minutes longer. Reduce the heat to low if the onions are turning dark brown.

Meanwhile, set an oven rack or broiler pan about 3 inches below the broiler and preheat the broiler. In a large bowl, whisk together the eggs and milk until thoroughly combined. Whisk in the parsley, dill, salt, and a few grinds of pepper. Set aside.

As soon as the potatoes are tender, add the egg mixture to the pan and stir in the salmon. Cook over medium–low heat until the frittata is set on the bottom and around the edges, about 4 minutes. While the frittata is cooking, use a spatula to lift one edge of the frittata and tilt the pan a little so some of the uncooked egg flows under the set edge. Repeat this at different places around the edge of the frittata.

When the eggs are mostly cooked, place the frittata under the broiler. Broil until the top is golden brown and the eggs are set but still moist, about 3 minutes. Allow the frittata to rest for 5 minutes, then slice in wedges and serve immediately.

Roasted Leek and Salmon Tartlets

Suggested wine: French red Burgundy; Oregon pinot noir

For entertaining, I love the look of individual tarts, whether sweet or savory. I think it makes a guest feel special to receive a tartlet rather than a slice. Though they may seem fussy to make, honestly they're not. There are so many do-ahead steps that it is a breeze for the host to have these hot from the oven without spending every moment in the kitchen. First, make the tartlet shells ahead and freeze them unbaked. Second, prebake the shells the morning of the brunch or lunch. Assemble and bake the tartlets 45 minutes before guests arrive, then reheat them just before serving. A salad or vegetable fills out the plate, making this a very special entrée.

MAKES EIGHT 4-INCH TARTLETS; SERVES 8 AS A MAIN COURSE

4 leeks, white and light green parts only, rinsed, cut into 1-inch lengths, and julienned

3 tablespoons extra-virgin olive oil

¾ teaspoon kosher or sea salt

Freshly ground pepper

3 large eggs

1¼ cups heavy (whipping) cream

1½ teaspoons minced fresh thyme

⅛ teaspoon freshly grated nutmeg

3 ounces soft herb and garlic cheese (such as Boursin or Cibo), at room temperature

1½ teaspoons fresh lemon juice

8 prebaked 4-inch tartlet shells *(recipe follows)*

3 ounces thinly sliced smoked salmon (lox), cut into bite-sized pieces

Set an oven rack in the center of the oven and preheat the oven to 400°F. Place the leeks in a 9-by-13-inch baking dish. Toss them with the olive oil, ¼ teaspoon of the salt, and a few grinds of pepper. Spread the leeks into a thin layer and roast, uncovered, stirring once, until tender and barely beginning to brown, about 20 minutes. Set aside.

CONTINUED

Meanwhile, in a medium bowl, whisk together the eggs, cream, thyme, nutmeg, the remaining $1/2$ teaspoon salt, and a few grinds of pepper. In a small bowl, blend together the cheese and lemon juice.

To assemble the tartlets, divide the leeks among the tartlet shells, scattering them over the bottom. Divide and arrange the salmon over the top. Place 3 separate teaspoonfuls of the cheese mixture on each tartlet. Give the cream mixture another stir, then carefully pour an equal amount into each tartlet shell, reserving about $1/2$ cup.

Bake the tartlets for 5 minutes, then remove from the oven. Pour the remaining cream mixture equally into each tartlet. Return the tartlets to the oven and bake until the custard is set, puffed, and golden on top, about 12 minutes longer. Place on a wire rack to cool for 5 minutes. Remove the tartlets from their pans and serve warm.

TARTLET SHELLS

3 cups all-purpose flour, plus more for rolling dough

1 teaspoon kosher or sea salt

1 cup (2 sticks) cold unsalted butter, cut into small cubes *(see Cook's Notes)*

About $1/2$ cup ice water

In a food processor fitted with the metal blade, add the 3 cups of flour and the salt. (See Cook's Notes for directions on making the pie dough by hand.) Pulse once or twice to mix. Scatter the butter over the flour and pulse several times until the butter is the size of small peas. With the machine running, add the ice water a little at a time just until the dough looks like it is coming together. Stop before it forms a ball. (You may not need all the water.)

Transfer the dough to a lightly floured work surface. Have ready eight 4-inch tart pans with removable bottoms. Using a rolling pin lightly dusted with flour, roll the dough into a large round about $1/8$ inch thick. Using a 6-inch bowl or plate as a template, cut out eight 6-inch circles. (You may need to reroll the dough to form the last 2 circles of dough.) Ease the dough into the bottom and sides of each tart pan, then press it gently in place. Fold the overhang over to form a double-thick crust along the sides. Run the rolling pin over the top to trim off any excess dough and make an even edge. Place the tartlet shells in the freezer for 30 minutes.

Position an oven rack in the center of the oven. Preheat the oven to 400°F. Place the tartlet shells on a large rimmed baking sheet. For each tartlet, prick the bottom of the crust with a fork, then place a piece of aluminum foil over the bottom of the crust and up the sides. Bake the crust for 10 minutes. Remove the foil and continue baking the crusts until set and just beginning to brown on the bottom and sides, 8 to 10 minutes longer. Transfer to a wire rack while making the filling.

MAKES EIGHT 4-INCH TARTLET SHELLS

COOK'S NOTES

To make the tartlet dough by hand, place the dry ingredients in a large bowl. Using a pastry blender or your fingertips, work the butter into the flour until it is the size of small peas. Add the ice water a little at a time, and stir with a fork just until the dough holds together. (You may not need all the water.) Flatten the dough into a disk ready to roll out. • One of the tricks I've learned from professional bakers is to freeze the flour and butter separately for about 20 minutes before making pastry. Everything gets very cold, which makes rolling out the dough much easier and keeps the pastry flaky.

Poached Eggs on Grilled Olive Bread
with Smoked Salmon

Suggested wine: Provençal rosé; dolcetto; Valpolicella

I think I could eat this recipe for brunch every Sunday and never get tired of it! I love the combination of an earthy rich tapenade mayonnaise smeared on a slice of grilled olive bread, topped with some smoked salmon and a perfectly poached egg. When you cut into the egg, the runny yolk soaks into the crusty bread. Each bite is a savory delight, especially with the addition of smoked salmon. No rich Hollandaise sauce is needed here. See the Cook's Notes for easy do-ahead preparations.

SERVES 4

6 tablespoons mayonnaise

3½ tablespoons minced fresh flat-leaf parsley

2 teaspoons store-bought or homemade black olive tapenade

Freshly ground pepper

Eight (¾-inch-thick) slices black or green olive ciabatta bread

Extra-virgin olive oil for brushing

16 slices thinly sliced smoked salmon (lox)

1 teaspoon distilled white vinegar or fresh lemon juice

1 teaspoon kosher or sea salt

8 large eggs

In a small bowl, combine the mayonnaise, 1½ tablespoons of the parsley, the tapenade, and a few grinds of pepper. Set aside.

Heat an indoor grill, grill pan, or ridged griddle until hot. Brush both sides of the bread with a little olive oil. Grill the bread on both sides until nice grill marks appear. Set aside.

Bring about 2 inches of water to a boil in a large sauté pan. While the water heats, spread each slice of grilled bread on one side with some of the prepared mayonnaise and then lay 2 slices of lox over the top. Arrange 2 slices on each of 4 warmed plates. Set aside.

When the water boils, add the vinegar or lemon juice and salt. Adjust the heat so the water is at a simmer, not a rolling boil. Crack each egg into a separate small bowl and slip them one at

a time into the water. After 2 or 3 minutes, use a slotted spoon to lift an egg to see whether the white has completely set. When it has, remove the eggs with a slotted spoon. Use kitchen shears or a paring knife to trim any ragged edges or "tails" from the whites of the eggs. Set 1 poached egg on each slice of prepared bread. Garnish each open-faced sandwich with a generous sprinkling of the remaining minced parsley and a couple of grinds of pepper. Serve immediately.

COOK'S NOTES

Some kitchen shops carry a little metal cup with feet and a vertical wire handle for poaching eggs. The little cup sits in the water and contains each egg in a perfect shape—crack the eggs directly into these forms if using them. • Poached eggs can easily be made up to 1 day in advance and then reheated. As soon as the eggs are cooked, slip them immediately into a bowl filled with cold water. Cover the bowl and refrigerate the eggs. To reheat, slip the eggs back into a pan filled with simmering water until heated through, less than 1 minute. (This is a great trick for entertaining.)

Spring Vegetable Potpie with Salmon

Suggested wine: French or California chardonnay; Beaujolais

This is such a great entrée for a brunch, lunch, or simple supper with friends because the potpies can be made a day in advance. Covered and refrigerated, they can go straight from the refrigerator to the oven to the table without last-minute cooking and fussing. I especially like to serve individual potpies when entertaining a group of 6 to 8. This recipe doubles easily.

SERVES 4

1 sheet frozen puff pastry dough, from a 17.3 ounce package

1½ cups dry white wine

1 large carrot, peeled, halved lengthwise, and thinly sliced

3 tablespoons unsalted butter

2 tablespoons vegetable oil

1 onion, diced

8 ounces chanterelle or cremini mushrooms, quartered

2 tablespoons all-purpose flour

½ cup heavy (whipping) cream

1 salmon fillet (1 pound), skin and pin bones removed (*see pages 30–33*), cut into ½-inch dice

½ cup fresh or frozen peas

2 tablespoons chopped fresh flat-leaf parsley

1 tablespoon chopped fresh dill

¾ teaspoon kosher or sea salt

¼ teaspoon freshly ground pepper

Remove the sheet of frozen puff pastry dough from its package and thaw at room temperature, about 25 minutes.

Preheat the oven to 400°F. Set four 12-ounce ramekins on a baking sheet, or use an 8-cup baking dish about 2 inches deep. (A 10-inch cast-iron skillet with 2-inch sides works great, too. You can make the filling right in the skillet.)

CONTINUED

Spring Vegetable Potpie with Salmon *continued*

TO MAKE THE FILLING: Bring the wine to a simmer in a small saucepan over medium-low heat. Add the carrots and cook until crisp-tender, 8 minutes. Using a slotted spoon, transfer the carrots to a plate and turn off the heat under the wine.

In a 10-inch skillet, preferably cast iron, melt the butter with the oil over medium heat until the butter foams. Add the onion and sauté until it begins to soften, about 2 minutes. Add the mushrooms and sauté until they just begin to brown, about 3 minutes longer. Sprinkle the flour over the onion mixture and stir to blend in. Slowly stir in the wine, bring to a simmer, and stir until smooth and thickened, about 2 minutes. Add the cream, stir to blend, and bring to a simmer. Add the salmon and cook just until it turns opaque, about 3 minutes. Add the peas, carrots, parsley, dill, salt, and pepper. Stir gently to combine. Taste and adjust the seasoning. Remove from the heat.

Divide the filling among the ramekins, spoon it into a baking dish, or leave it in the cast-iron skillet you cooked the filling in. Unfold the sheet of pastry and lay it flat on a lightly floured work surface. For individual potpies, roll out the pastry to a 12-inch square. Using a 5- or 6-inch plate, cut out 4 rounds. Cut two 2-inch-long slits in the center of each round. For 1 large potpie, roll out the pastry to an 11-inch square, trimming the edges with a paring knife to form a circle. Cut three 2-inch-long slits in the center of the dough. Carefully place the dough over the filling, centering it. Firmly press the edges of the dough against the sides of the ramekins or the pan. Bake until the dough is nicely browned and puffed, about 25 minutes. Serve immediately.

COOK'S NOTE

The salmon potpies can be prepared up to 1 day in advance and baked just before serving. Cover tightly and refrigerate. (This is not recommended if you are using a cast-iron skillet, though an enamel-lined, cast-iron skillet would be fine.) Allow about 40 minutes for the potpies to bake.

Smoked Salmon, Onion, and Arugula Quiche

Suggested wine: French or California chardonnay; Beaujolais

Certain dishes defy food trends, and I think quiches are one of them, mostly because they taste and look so good. Who can resist a buttery-rich flaky crust and a savory filling packed with flavor? I can't. This quiche is no exception, and it makes a terrific brunch or lunch dish. Sautéed onion slices are scattered over the bottom of a prebaked crust topped with goat cheese, smoked salmon, and a mound of peppery arugula. When the custard filling is fully baked, the edges are puffed with a golden glow, and hints of pink salmon and leaves of green streak across the top, making this tart artful as well as delicious.

MAKES ONE 9-INCH QUICHE; SERVES 6

1 tablespoon olive oil

1 cup thinly sliced onion

1 prebaked 9-inch pie crust *(recipe follows)*

3 ounces fresh goat cheese, crumbled

2 ounces thinly sliced smoked salmon (lox), cut into 1-inch pieces

¾ cup firmly packed arugula leaves, stemmed

2 large eggs

1 large egg yolk

1 cup heavy (whipping) cream

½ teaspoon kosher or sea salt

Pinch of freshly grated nutmeg

Freshly ground pepper

Position an oven rack in the center of the oven. Preheat the oven to 375°F.

In a small sauté pan, heat the olive oil over medium-high heat and swirl to coat the pan. Add the onion and sauté, stirring frequently, until softened and just beginning to brown, about 5 minutes. Set aside to cool for 5 minutes.

CONTINUED

Scatter the onion over the bottom of the prebaked crust. Scatter the cheese and salmon over the top. Distribute the arugula evenly in the quiche. (It will seem like there is too much arugula, but it will flatten once the cream mixture is added.) In a medium bowl, whisk the eggs and egg yolk together until well beaten, then whisk in the cream. Add the salt, nutmeg, and a couple grinds of pepper and whisk again. Pour this mixture over the quiche filling, being careful not to go over the sides of the crust. Press down any arugula that is not covered by the cream mixture. Bake the quiche until slightly puffed and lightly browned at the edges, 25 to 30 minutes. Remove from the oven and let stand for 10 minutes before serving.

PIE CRUST

2 cups all-purpose flour, plus more for rolling dough

½ teaspoon kosher or sea salt

½ cup (1 stick) plus 2 tablespoons cold unsalted butter, cut into small cubes

About ⅓ cup ice water

In a food processor fitted with the metal blade, combine the 2 cups flour and the salt. (See Cook's Notes, page 179, for directions on making pie dough by hand.) Pulse once or twice to mix. Scatter the butter over the flour and pulse several times until the butter is the size of small peas. With the machine running, add the ice water a little at a time just until the dough looks like it is coming together. Stop before it forms a ball. (You may not need all the water.)

Transfer the dough to a lightly floured work surface. Using a rolling pin lightly dusted with flour, roll the dough into an 11-inch round. Drape the dough over the rolling pin and carefully transfer it to a 9-inch tart pan with a removable bottom. Ease the dough into the bottom and sides of the pan, press it gently in place, and trim the overhang to $3/4$ inch. Fold the overhang over to form a double–thick crust along the sides. Run the rolling pin over the top to trim off any excess dough and make an even edge. Place the tart shell in the freezer for 30 minutes.

Position an oven rack in the center of the oven. Preheat the oven to 400°F. Prick the bottom of the crust with a fork. Place a piece of aluminum foil or parchment paper over the bottom of the crust and up the sides. Fill it with pie weights, dried beans, or rice. Bake the crust for 12 minutes. Remove the foil or parchment along with the weights. Continue baking the crust until set and just beginning to brown on the bottom and sides, 10 minutes longer. Transfer to a wire rack while making the filling.

MAKES ONE 9-INCH PIE CRUST

KITCHEN EQUIPMENT, STOVETOP SMOKERS, WOOD CHIPS

Sur La Table
1765 Sixth Avenue South
Seattle, Washington 98134
800-243-0852
surlatable.com

Cooking.com
800-663-8810

Cameronssmoker.com
888-563-0227

Chinook Planks
Chinookplanks.com
800-765-4408

WILD AND WILD CAUGHT SALMON

Copper River Seafoods
P.O. Box 158
Cordova, Alaska 99574
888-622-1197
copperriverseafood.com

Fisherman Direct Seafoods
P.O. Box 547
Gold Beach, Oregon 97444
888-523-9494
FishermanDirect.com

Alaska Harvest Seafood
5773 SE International Way
Portland, Oregon 97222
800-824-6389
alaskaharvest.com

EcoFish, Inc.
EcoFish, 78 Market Street,
Portsmouth, New Hampshire 03801
603-430-0101
fax: 603-430-9929
ecofish.com

SCOTTISH QUALITY SALMON

Wester Ross Salmon, Ltd.
Ullapool, Ross-shire, Scotland IV26 2TN
+44 (0)1463-713371
fax: +44 (0)1463-712144
email: sales@wrs.co.uk

SMOKED SALMON

*Great American Smokehouse
and Seafood Company*
Harbor, Oregon 97415
800-828-FISH (3474)
Smokehouse-salmon.com

SeaBear Smokehouse
605 30th Street
P.O. Box 591
Anacortes, Washington
800-645-3474
seabear.com

Max & Me Catering
4723 Durham Road
Doylestown, Pennsylvania 18901
800-503-3663
maxandmeinc.com

Zabar's
2245 Broadway
New York, New York 10024
212-787-2000
Zabars.com

Kinvara Smoked Salmon Ltd.
Ireland
+353-91-637-489
Kinvarasmokedsalmon.com

SOURCES

INDEX

The exact equivalents in the following tables have been rounded for convenience.

LIQUID/DRY MEASURES

U.S.	Metric
1/4 teaspoon	1.25 milliliters
1/2 teaspoon	2.5 milliliters
1 teaspoon	5 milliliters
1 tablespoon (3 teaspoons)	15 milliliters
1 fluid ounce (2 tablespoons)	30 milliliters
1/4 cup	60 milliliters
1/3 cup	80 milliliters
1/2 cup	120 milliliters
1 cup	240 milliliters
1 pint (2 cups)	480 milliliters
1 quart (4 cups, 32 ounces)	960 milliliters
1 gallon (4 quarts)	3.84 liters
1 ounce (by weight)	28 grams
1 pound	454 grams
2.2 pounds	1 kilogram

LENGTH

U.S.	Metric
1/8 inch	3 millimeters
1/4 inch	6 millimeters
1/2 inch	12 millimeters
1 inch	2.5 centimeters

OVEN TEMPERATURES

Fahrenheit	Celsius	Gas
250	120	1/2
275	140	1
300	150	2
325	160	3
350	180	4
375	190	5
400	200	6
425	220	7
450	230	8
475	240	9
500	260	10

TABLE OF EQUIVALENTS